C000104612

LIVERPOOL'S CHILDREN

IN THE SECOND WORLD WAR

LIVERPOOL'S CHILDREN

IN THE SECOND WORLD WAR

PAMELA RUSSELL

This book is for my husband, David, my son, Christopher, and my daughter-in law, Sarah, all of whom are post-war Liverpool children. Also for my brother-in-law, Harold Russell, and my cousin, Brenda Bryce, née Wright, both of whom were Liverpool children in the Second World War.

Pamela Russell (M.Phil.) is a retired Senior Lecturer of Edge Hill University, Ormskirk, Lancashire. She has lived in Maghull, Walton and, for over thirty years, Lydiate.

First published 2009

The History Press
The Mill, Brimscombe Port
Stroud, Gloucestershire, GL5 2QG
www.thehistorypress.co.uk

Reprinted 2010

© Pamela Russell, 2009

The right of Pamela Russell to be identified as the Author
of this work has been asserted in accordance with the
Copyrights, Designs and Patents Act 1988.

All rights reserved. No part of this book may be reprinted
or reproduced or utilised in any form or by any electronic,
mechanical or other means, now known or hereafter invented,
including photocopying and recording, or in any information
storage or retrieval system, without the permission in writing
from the Publishers.

British Library Cataloguing in Publication Data.
A catalogue record for this book is available from the British Library.

ISBN 978 0 7524 5158 9

Typesetting and origination by The History Press
Printed and bound in Great Britain by
Marston Book Services Limited, Didcot

Contents

Acknowledgements

My thanks to all the people who wrote to me with their stories of their wartime child-hood, or lent photographs. James Abram, on behalf of Winifred Abram; Victoria Bradford, on behalf of Joan Stables; Linda Leaworthy, on behalf of Stan Lewis and Renee Rose; Mrs J.M. Taylor, on behalf of Phil Taylor.

Mr W. Backshall
Mrs M.E. Barber
Mrs E. Barooah
Mrs M. Bentley
Mr A. Bentley
Mr F. Berwick
Mrs P. Blamire
Mr B.F. Browne
Mr R. Brundrit
Mrs B. Bryce
Mr D. Buckley
Mrs P. Burns
Mrs J. Campbell
Mrs A. Chapman
Mrs E. Charles
Mrs I. Collinson
Mr W. Courtliffe
Mr R.A. Cox
Mrs M. Crimmins
Mr G. Crompton
Mr H. Croston
Mrs D. Dalrymple
Mrs E. Davies
Mr D.E. Davies
Mrs E. Doyle
Mrs P. Fawcett
Mr D. Ferguson
Mr D. Finney
Mr A.E. Forster

Mr H. Gaskell
Mrs J. Gillett
Mr A.P. Graham
Mr A. Gahan
Mr T. Grayson
Mrs J. Greenhalgh
Mrs M. Greenwood
Mr J. Greer
Mr G. Halligan
Mrs M. Hardman
Mrs A. Harrison
Mrs B. Harrison
Mr D. Hartley-Backhouse
Mr B. Hefferan
Mr B. Hill
Mrs M. Hoban
Mr F. Holcroft
Mrs D.M. Hudson
Mr D. Hunter
Mrs J. Ireland
Mrs F. Jennings
Mr J. Johnson
Mrs E.A. Johnston
Mrs J. Jones
Mrs K. Kenyon
Mrs S. Landrum
Mrs P. Lawrenson
Mr A. Lewis
Mrs M. Luke

Mrs P. Martin
Mrs R. McArt
Mrs T. McAsey
Mr P. McGuinness
Mrs J. MacLeod
Miss J. McMurtry
Mr J. McMurtry
Mr J. Middleton
Mr R. Molyneux
Mrs S. Moonan
Mrs J. Morley
Mr F. Nelson
Mr A. Parks
Mrs S. Part
Mrs B. Patten
Mr B. Pearson
Mr R.J. Pedersen
Mrs D. Pemberton
Mrs B. Redfern
Mrs P. Rider
Mr R. Rigby
Mr B. Riley
Mr S. Roberts
Mr P. Robinson
Mr D. Rusling
Mr H. Russell
Miss M Ryman

Mrs M. Salthouse
Mrs D. Scott
Mrs O. Serridge
Mrs P. Sharkey
Mrs M. Sheehan
Ms P.A. Silcock
Mrs G. Skinner
Mr V. Smith
Miss L.G. Smith
Mr F. Smith
Miss I. Stephenson
Mrs E. Sweeney
Mrs J. Taylor
Mrs J. Tisdale
Mr P.D. Walker
Mr B. Webb
Mr T.E. Wells
Mr L. Whittaker
Mr A. Williams
Mr J. Williams
Mr M. Wilson
Mr T. Wood
Mrs O.L. Woods
Mrs M. Wrench
Mrs P. Whittington Richardson
Mrs B. Yorke

Photographs and Illustrations

Thanks to my husband, David Russell, without whose technical and photographic expertise none of these photographs and illustrations would have appeared at all.

Photographs and illustrations appear courtesy of: Vic Smith, Pam Fawcett and Gillian Skinner; Christopher Russell; Diane Courtney of UK Good Housekeeping and the National Magazine Company; Anne Gleave and National Museums Liverpool (Merseyside Maritime Museum); The Stewart Bale Collection; Mark Sargent and the Local History Unit, South Sefton, Sefton Library Service and The Imperial War Museum.

Introduction

This is the story of Liverpool's children during the Second World War. It is a real attempt to tell the full story and to include as many people's memories as possible, told in their own words. Included are numerous aspects of life in wartime, as they affected children at the time. Many of the people who have contacted me have never told the story of their experience before. Most of them make light of the less happy aspects of those times, even when they are recounting quite sad or frightening events. Almost all the stories told or sent to me include some humorous or light-hearted anecdotes, which have been included to illustrate that most children will usually rise above the worst of times. Liverpool's children in the war years did not lose the sense of humour for which the city is justifiably famous. It is clear that the desire 'not to whine' which was adopted by many of the children has become a lifelong habit for many of the war's younger generation.

At the same time, there has been an eagerness and an enthusiasm about the opportunity to tell their stories. Sometimes there was surprise that anyone is interested, suggesting that a great deal has been 'bottled up' for too long and for a whole host of reasons – personal pride, patriotism, consideration for others and, perhaps, the simple desire to forget such a confusing and complex part of childhood.

Marguerite Patten OBE, in her commentary on some aspects of the war experience for Channel 4's *The 1940s House*, points out that many people did not want to talk about the difficulties and fears of those years in their immediate aftermath. They just wanted to forget. By the time they were ready to talk, there was, for most people, no one to tell. This was particularly true for children. The general view then was that children should not be allowed to 'dwell on things' – they should be kept busy and 'would soon forget'. But they did not forget.

In fact, the memories of those years are sharp and fresh and surprisingly detailed. This book began with the younger people who are interested in the experiences of the children of the war years in mind, but as it progressed, it became increasingly apparent that the re-telling of those times was a good experience for many of the narrators as well as for their audience.

The personal stories that appear throughout this book were responses to my request in the press for the wartime memories of people who were children in Liverpool during Second World War. Childhood has been defined for this purpose as under the age of eighteen in September 1939, and born before September 1945. In the grammar schools, sixth-formers could be eighteen years old and evacuated with their schools to the reception areas.

However, for many children in 1939, school leaving age was fourteen years old. Young people who were already in jobs and bringing home a wage did not see themselves as children and, in any case, would not have been included in the schools scheme for evacuation. So there were distinctions and wide differences between the experiences of people of the same age. An article in the *Liverpool Echo* of 2 May 1941 carried the headline:

Tony's Travels
Youngest Merchant Seaman

It tells of:

Anthony Dowland of 62, Great Newton Street, 14 last March, serving as a barber-boy and mess-boy on a Holland-American Line Ship… 'I like seeing and going places' he told the *Echo*, drawing himself up to his full 4 feet 5 1/2 inches. Tony has five brothers in the Army and one brother killed in the recent air raids.

A recurring phrase in people's accounts of their wartime childhood years was 'You just got used to it!'. This seemed to encapsulate what many of the people have said of the air raids, bereavement, hardship or absence from home and parents, 'You just got used to it', 'You became accustomed to it' or 'It became our idea of "normal". This stoical and matter-of-fact attitude to the various events of a wartime childhood has often been seen as just one aspect of those very different times. And it is clear that children wanted to play their part in supporting parents, especially their mothers when fathers were absent. The children could see how very brave their parents were being themselves. Children who stayed at home often became very close to their mothers in a mutually supportive way and many people have expressed their appreciation for the efforts that their parents made to give them as 'normal' a childhood, with all its little treats, as was humanly possible in the circumstances.

However, it is also apparent that children were encouraged to display 'a stiff upper lip' from a very young age. In 1939, the *British Movietone News*, shown in cinemas, had an item showing pictures of planes, warships, men digging trenches in the parks for air-raid shelters and children boarding trains and buses for evacuation, with this hearty 'voice-over':

War has been declared, but our Forces have been mobilised and are ready to stand firm against the Nazi aggressor. No-one wants to go down this path again, but Britain is ready to dig in for the fight and our children steadfastly play their part on the road to Victory. 'God speed and you'll soon be home again!'

This rousing encouragement to the whole nation was reinforced locally and aimed directly at the children. In the *Liverpool Echo* of 23 March 1940, 'Auntie's Letter Bag', a column that encouraged children to send in their contributions to the paper for publication, begins:

Dear Boys and Girls, – In sending contributions, would you try and enclose *cheerful* articles for your stories and poems. Sometimes the work is good, but too doleful for our page.

The story that was published entitled 'The Evacuees' Adventure' was written by Joan Greenough of Claremont Road, Sefton Park, a pupil at Arundel Central School. We are not told whether Joan was an evacuee, only her home address is given, but the story begins 'Jill and Jane were evacuated to North Wales… they were both Guides, so they decided to go to a company in their district in North Wales.' As the story unfolds, the two girls help to secure the capture of two burglars. The story ends 'These two little Guides were the pride of their company, and they said that it wasn't so bad being away from home when you had such adventures.'

This story was almost certainly approved and published because it was upbeat and cheerful, but also because it included the sensible idea that familiar activities, such as Scouts, Guides, Wolf Cubs and Brownies, continued in unfamiliar surroundings, would offer a framework of stability for children who were living away from home. And, of course, one of the Guide Laws 'A Guide smiles and sings under all difficulties' would be approved by an editorial concept that discouraged 'doleful' correspondence.

But evacuation was, for many, a brief interlude. Less than a week after Joan's story appeared, the *Liverpool Echo* of 28 March 1940 carried the headline:

More City Schools to Reopen
Big Extension Announced
Liverpool List of Fifty-Six
Shelters Ready
Half –time Attendance in Most Cases
Start in April

Despite the great pressure on parents to send their children out of the cities and towns – and equally great pressure on country folk to take children into their homes – only six months after the war began, there were sufficient numbers of children in Liverpool to reopen the doors of fifty-six more schools 'for the first time since the closure enforced by the war'. This brought 'the total of Liverpool schools affording educational facilities to 112... just 60% of the total number of schools normally in occupation throughout the city'.

Of course, the closure of schools had just been one aspect of the official expectation that parents would send their children out of the city. And there was still an undertone of pressure on parents and disapproval of those whose children remained in the family home:

> ...it must be remembered that it is still the view of the Government and the local authority that children should remain in the reception areas... As was explained to the *Echo*, the primary consideration is the safety of the children, but, *if parents are prepared to take the risks*, the Education Committee *will do their best to provide shelters in the schools.*

There have been other books about child evacuation, but little or nothing about children who stayed at home or other aspects of a child's experience of war. Most of the people who have attempted to document this period have put great emphasis on the mass evacuation of children from the cities. For instance, the Reader's Digest publication *Yesterday's Britain* suggests that 'Another very tangible sign that Britain was at war, was the absence of children from towns and cities'.

The belief that the towns and cities of Britain were emptied of children is, in many ways, a myth. Certainly, for Liverpool it was a myth. In my own family, older cousins had not been involved in evacuation. Many children never left the city at any time. Many families stayed together. And many of those children who were evacuated soon returned, sometimes within a few days or a couple of weeks. The Christmas of 1939 saw many children come home and never return to their foster homes. Some children went away for a time and then came home, because it was not until 17 August 1940 that the first bombs were dropped on Liverpool. However, many children were evacuated for a second time, and even a third time, especially during or immediately after the Christmas raids of 1940 and the ferocious Blitz of May 1941. This group are those I have called 'the yo-yo children'. Some children did stay away for the whole period of the war, but these appear to be a small minority.

Mass evacuation, organised by the authorities through the schools, is the most documented and the most emotionally dramatic form of evacuation, because of the separation of parents and children. Parents did not know their children's destination and the luggage labels attached to crocodiles of children, some tearful, some stoic, some innocently excited, tend to catch the imagination. Such scenes have come to be seen by later generations as 'what happened to children in the war.'

But this was not the only way in which children went to live in safer areas. Some children went to stay with relations in the country or in 'safer' towns. Other children were among the 'trekkers', who left Liverpool nightly for the surrounding areas, such as the inland parishes of Maghull and Lydiate. Some people who left Liverpool each night went to stay with relatives, returning each morning hoping that their home was still standing. Although there were some lorries laid on to take people out of the city to safer areas, there were also some 'trekkers' who just set off to walk away from the danger, preferring to sleep under hedgerows rather than stay in the city. In the event, many were taken in on an *ad hoc* basis by local people, and church and parish halls were also opened to take them in. One Maghull resident wondered why Lydiate's Grayson Memorial Hall seemed so familiar, until she was told by an elderly aunt that she had slept there as a very young child for a number of nights during the May Blitz of 1941, when her family had 'trekked' from their home in Bootle.

This book aims to tell a complete story of all the children of Liverpool during the Second World War, not just the story of evacuation, which was just one, albeit dramatic, aspect of the whole picture. Of course, there will always be someone's story that has not been told. But these graphic accounts do cover most aspects of children's lives in wartime. So far as possible, I have allowed the children to speak for themselves and have set their stories in the context of the events of those times. The experience of total war is seen and recounted from the point of view of the Home Front and, more particularly, through the eyes and ears of children. They were powerless then, but now, I hope, they have been given a voice.

Chapter One

War 'breaks out'

Children realised that something was amiss with their world in a variety of ways.

Bernard Browne left Liverpool's landing stage with his parents and three-year-old-sister for Douglas and their usual week's holiday on the Isle of Man on Saturday 26 August 1939. Bernard was eleven years old. He recalls:

> The week's holiday went well following its usual care-free style until Friday 1 September, when the news broke that Germany had invaded Poland… as was the custom of our family we were visiting the main shopping area buying bits and pieces for our return home… including a beautiful box of Manx kippers. This Friday morning was different; hundreds of people were gathered outside some of the shops which had their radios turned on to the events of the day.

When war was actually declared on Sunday 3 September, Bernard remembers his mother 'crying her eyes out and terribly distressed'. It was explained to him later that his mother's brother, a Sergeant in the Royal Horse Artillery, had been killed in France in 1917.

The First World War had ended only twenty-one years before in 1918, and few adults had escaped without losing at least one family member. So it was still very close and the dread of its huge losses may explain why so many people found it difficult to believe that it could happen again, and why they shielded children until it was impossible to keep them in ignorance any longer. Indeed, the phrase 'war broke out', used so often by the generation of adults of that time, suggests a predatory beast that could scarcely be contained. Some parents had deliberately protected children from knowledge of the coming upheaval. Perhaps they thought that it might never happen. Certainly, many hoped right up to the beginning of the war that it could not possibly happen. Most parents tried to carry on a normal lifestyle right up to the declaration of war, even going on holiday that week, like Bernard's family. Besides the natural desire of parents to protect them, children in most families in the 1930s were not so aware of events in the adult world as children are today.

Nevertheless, various circumstances or events impinged on children's lives and made them increasingly aware of the situation. Some children were so young that they became aware very gradually that changes were taking place around them. Maureen Burrows, three in 1939, noticed that 'the adults seemed very serious and were always listening to the radio'.

Older children, who visited the cinema, were more likely to have seen the news-reels, which were shown at every performance. Reg Cox, born in 1929 and living in Ferndale Road, near Greenbank Park, had 'frequently seen images of the German Army marching across yet another country, masses of troops and columns of tanks smashing all before them'. Children with older brothers and sisters were also more aware of impending war. Reg, for instance, was aware of the coming conflict because his sister, Pat, signed on in the Women's Auxiliary Air Force (WAAF) in the summer of 1939. Reg also noted the absence of a German classmate after the school holidays of summer 1939:

> At the Morrison School, near Greenbank Park, one of my classmates was a German lad, Heinz Garke; his father worked in some office in Liverpool. I was quite friendly with Heinz and was a bit miffed when he didn't turn up after the Summer Holidays. No doubt his family were told to return to the Fatherland… Heinz probably wound up in the 'Hitler Youth'.

James Middleton, born in 1931, witnessed an unusual sight during the last summer holiday before the war:

> It was in the school holidays in the summer of 1939. My younger sister and I along with a playmate walked a mile or so to Huyton Village to buy a twopenny packet of foreign stamps (obviously not rarities). On the way back, we sat on the wall of the village pub to inspect our purchase but we were interrupted by this strange sight. Walking down the village street was a column of people, mostly men but some women, carrying suitcases or bags, many of them having coats over their arms (it was a warm day). The column was flanked by soldiers shouldering rifles with fixed bayonets. Although we were very young, we understood a little of the international situation through the news bulletins on the radio ('wireless' as we called it in those days).

James explains this incident:

> Following the Fall of France in 1940, thousands of foreign nationals living in Britain (Germans, Austrians, Italians etc.)… were rounded up and put into internment camps, one of which was in Huyton where I lived as a child. This camp was actually an uncompleted council housing estate. However, I suspect that 'enemy aliens' were being interned in the weeks leading up to the outbreak of war.

The official report on Huyton Internment Camp does suggest that it was established in 1940. It may be, however, that James, his sister and his friend witnessed some early arrivals. It was believed that foreign nationals, such as Germans, Austrians and Italians, posed a threat to national security and there were several such camps, set up under military guards, to restrict the movement and contact of such people. Although there was undoubtedly espionage at that time, the sad irony was that many of the internees were intellectual or artistic refugees from Nazism, who continued their educational activities amongst themselves in the camp, earning it the nickname of 'Huyton University'.

Also in 1939, many children were puzzled when workmen began to dig up the parks where they went to play. Other children suddenly found that their back garden no longer had much space in it for games. Air-raid precautions were being put in place.

In 1938, Neville Chamberlain placed Sir John Anderson in charge of Air Raid Precautions (ARP). The engineer, William Patterson, was commissioned by Anderson to design a small shelter for mass production that could be erected in people's gardens. Some records suggest that the Anderson shelter was actually designed by Dr David Anderson and is named after him, and not after the Home Secretary. Nearly 1.5 million Anderson shelters were distributed. They comprised six curved sheets of corrugated iron bolted together at the top, with steel plates at each end. They measured 6ft 6ins by 4ft 6ins and were meant for six people. The shelters were to be half-buried in the ground with earth piled on top. The entrance was meant to be protected by a steel shield and a bank of earth as a blast wall. They had disadvantages. In low-lying areas or in wet weather, they tended to flood. They did not keep out the deafening noise of an air raid. They also depended on the competence of the people who erected them for their effectiveness. Some were installed well, with some attempt at drainage. Many people grew vegetables on top of them as a simple form of camouflage and extra insulation against the winter nights. Men who earned less than £250 per year, approximately £5 per week, were issued with a free shelter, while those who earned more could buy one for £7. By September 1940, 2.3 million had been distributed, but in May of that year, the newspapers were carrying warnings that shelters must be erected by June, or an explanation would be required by the local council.

Not all air-raid shelters were 'standard issue'. Although the Wirral was considered a safe enough area to receive evacuees, people living there still felt safer with the protection of an air-raid shelter. Patricia Blamire, née Collinge, lived in Meols and was ten in 1939:

> As our house had been built on the original sand dunes, it was a simple matter for my father to excavate a space in the garden large enough to hold a shelter, so he built a wooden structure and covered it with sods, where we spent many nights, whilst poor father varied his nights between fire-watching at the office in Liverpool and Home Guard duties in Meols. We were lucky because although the Luftwaffe flew regularly overhead, there was only an occasional BOMB dropped. I remember the excitement of viewing the crater on Hoylake promenade.

It is clear that the dropping of a bomb was a rare and exciting occurrence that still warrants the use of capital letters, though, for Patricia, not necessarily very frightening. It is tempting to assume that this was because Patricia was a safe distance from the most dangerous areas. However, it also seems likely that some parents had the gift of making their children feel safe in the midst of the worst experiences.

Joyce Morley was ten-and-a-half in May 1941 and lived in Childwall. Perhaps because her family moved to Childwall only a fortnight before war was declared, and she was in the process of changing schools, Joyce was not evacuated. She comments:

> Although what became known as the 'May Blitz' was so long ago, I remember clearly how life was for me as a child in a Liverpool suburb. I realise now that it was a savage onslaught and many people were killed yet, despite the drone of German planes above, the whistle of bombs, the bright flashes as land-mines reached their targets and the noise of Ack-ack guns fighting off the enemy, I was never really frightened and am ashamed to say that my brother and I probably found it rather exciting. We had a child-like faith that because Mum and Dad were there, we would be quite safe and no bomb could possibly hit our house. Hmm!

Joyce remembers her family's attempts to find shelter during the May Blitz:

> There were humorous incidents, of course, despite the seriousness. Most of ours arose out of my father's inability to erect a private air-raid shelter he had bought. We were not entitled to a free Anderson shelter, because he was slightly over the income for eligibility. Ours consisted of curved concrete slabs, which sat, unmade up, all through those shocking nights and forced us to seek out other places to shelter within the house. Under the stairs was shelter Number One. A tiny, tiny cubby-hole which had me and my brother squabbling because his knees were always sticking in my back. From time to time, after a huge flash, my parents would dive on top of us, causing more squeals and yells. Dad couldn't tolerate our fighting and moved us to 'safe zone' Number Two – a single storey wash kitchen. Because shrapnel could have pierced the tiled roof, he had us all sitting there with saucepans on our heads. I ask you… what would we have looked like if we had had to be dug out of the rubble. At first, Dad thought that not

having much house above us would be safer, but he changed his mind again and we ended up under a sturdy dining table with a mattress against the windows to protect us from breaking glass. We could even listen to Tommy Handley on the radio.

Joyce goes on:

One night, there was a mix-up with the air-raid sirens. They sounded the 'All-Clear' when they should not have done. Thankful to stretch his long legs, Dad got up from under the table and we followed. He poured himself a glass of milk stout and had just taken a large swig when there was an almighty bang as a bomb fell nearby. A huge spume of stout shot out of each side of his mouth like an enormous moustache, sending us children into fits of laughter and still is a source of merriment today. The next 'safe zone', following the table, was a brick-built public shelter round the corner in Taggart Avenue. So, clutching blankets and pillows, we trudged to the shelter, where many neighbours were. This was far more dangerous as shrapnel was coming down like confetti. Of course, there was a total black-out and mother managed to mistake a complete stranger passing the gate for my father. She took hold of him and whispered in the startled man's ear! Afterwards, she told us that she'd asked him to dash upstairs and get her teeth that she'd left soaking!

The public shelter wasn't right, so the next night, the last of the May Blitz, dad said we would all stop in our own beds, which, by now, were downstairs, except for my brother's. That night, we heard a frightening swishing sound and smelt burning. Terrified at what they might see, Mum and Dad went upstairs and there, embedded in my brother's bed, was the nose-cap of a shell. Mercifully, he had not yet gone to bed. Eventually, my Dad found someone to put the shelter up. We used it once during a later raid. After about an hour and a half, we felt water lapping around our ankles. It had been built over a spring! After the war, it was covered over and became a flower bed. I wonder whether the people who bought our house know what that funny mound was once?

Bernard Browne's family had returned home early from their Isle of Man holiday to find that the blackout, which 'shocked and horrified' Bernard, was already in force. In order to make it difficult for German pilots to find their targets, at the outbreak of war the British government imposed a total blackout. Everyone had to ensure that they did not show any light that would suggest to German air-crews that they were passing over a built-up area. Thick black curtains and blackout paint was used. Doors of shops and houses were not to be opened in a manner that allowed light to show from within. Even the light from a cigarette or match was forbidden. People were fined for any infringement and the Air Raid Warden's cry 'Put that light out!' became a rueful joke. Despite the humour in Joyce Morley's memory of her mother mistaking a stranger for her husband, it does illustrate how the darkness was frighteningly all-enveloping. Most people felt that the darkness was one of the real hardships of wartime and a dampener of their spirits. One of the great pleasures of peace was the end of the blackout and the freedom to sit with open curtains to 'show a light' from lamp or fire.

Jean Campbell, ten in November 1939, left school at fourteen in 1943 and went to work in Owen Owen, which was a large and popular department store in Clayton Square, 'I remember going to work and falling off the tram. It was dark.'

Like Jean, many people were hurt in the all-enveloping darkness. Kerb edges were painted white, but people fell on uneven surfaces or walked into lamp-posts or other obstacles and bombing had meant that, at times, there was debris everywhere. Cars could show no lights, or dipped and shielded lights, and the number of people killed on the roads almost doubled, despite the fact that there were fewer cars on the roads because many car owners had no fuel to use their vehicles.

Shirley Landrum, née Warbrick, was five in 1939, with a baby sister, Glenda, four years younger. Shirley lived on the outskirts of Liverpool, at Roby. She remembers very clearly for such a little girl:

> One day Dad and the old man next door, Mr Hesketh, dug a big hole in our garden. They put together pieces of corrugated iron and made a small metal hut. Half of it went round the sides of the hole and the rest, above ground, was covered with soil. This was our air raid shelter. Inside the floor was flattened earth. Half was used for a plank bed for me and Glenda; along the rest of the wall space were two wooden benches for grown-ups to sit on. The doorway had a piece of sacking dropped over it, weighted down with a length of wood nailed on to stop it blowing about. When the siren sounded in the night, Mr Hesketh carried me from our house and Mum carried Glenda. We were both rolled in blankets. No bedding could be left in the shelter – it would be too damp. We slept on the plank bed. Mrs. Hesketh and Mum tried to knit by the oil lamp light. I think Mr Hesketh thought he had to look after all of us, Dad being a fireman.

This seems to be a case of neighbourly co-operation. Mr Hesketh was an old man, and it seems likely that he could not dig out the ground for his Anderson shelter alone. Shirley's father was younger but, as a fireman, would not be there to help his wife with the two young children when air raids took place. So they erected one shelter and shared it. They helped each other, as many of the people who have told their stories have described.

Shirley was one of those children who were protected from too much awareness of the danger by the adults. She says that, 'More than once, we had been to the shelter in the night and because the grown-ups were careful never to frighten us with the war, we slept right through and woke up next morning in our beds.'

Like Shirley, whose father was in the Fire Service, David Ferguson was one of those children whose domestic world changed very little, and so he was secure and relatively unafraid. David lived at No. 3, Nook Rise in Wavertree Garden Suburb and was four years old at the beginning of the war:

> My father had a job which exempted him from having to join any of the Services… he was quite upset at not being called up and he felt guilty at not doing his bit for the country. At least he did something on the Home Front – he was an air-raid warden. I was only four years old when war broke out and used to sleep through the air raids even when sirens were blasting out and the Ack-Ack guns were fired at the enemy planes and the bombs were exploding. Even as I got older I don't remember being frightened and used to look out of the windows… to see what was going on until my Mum told me to get some clothes on and go down to the shelter in the back garden. We only used the shelter a couple of times as it was cold and damp so Mum, Jean (his sister, two years older) and myself (Dad was on duty fire-watching) used to go under the stairs until the all-clear sounded. Later, dad fitted out our coal place with bunks and we used to sleep there each night. It was quite cosy.

Peter McGuiness was also four years old in 1939, and lived in Bootle. Like David and Shirley, his home life was not completely disrupted, because Peter's father was a docker, a reserved occupation. So the family stayed together. At first, Peter:

> Naturally, did not understand what was going on. The bombing did not frighten me and the consequences of a German invasion never crossed my mind… when I started to understand the situation in about 1942, when I was seven, the allies were winning the war. In fact, I never remember a time when I did not think that we would win.

Unlike David and Peter, the outbreak of war was brought home to Francis (Nick) Nelson, born in June 1931 and living in Fairfield, in no uncertain terms:

> My father was in the Royal Air Force Voluntary Reserve and, in August 1939, he went on summer camp. Needless to say, he was not released! War started on the 3rd of September, and he stayed 'on camp'. I can recall hearing the radio announcement of the Declaration of War and paperboys running round the streets selling special editions of the *Echo*. Prior to this, I can recall in the summer of 1939 in Sheil Park, a barrage balloon site and the balloon in the air. The location was behind the old Cosy Cinema on Boaler Street.

It must have made the war very real to a little boy of eight, when his father went to the usual camp and was not allowed to return home.

Muriel Wrench, née Eskrigge, was twelve in January 1939. Her extended family lived in Ewart Road, Seaforth, where her father and his brother ran a refrigeration and cold storage company from No. 19, and also owned Nos 13, 15 and 17, which had been built by Muriel's grandfather, a builder. Muriel's family lived a comfortable existence with a grandmother, uncles, aunts and cousins living nearby or visited on holidays. Muriel had stayed with relatives in Scotland early in August 1939, 'I travelled back to Liverpool alone. Auntie Joan put me in the care of a respectable-looking lady – I remember she was very kind and took me to the restaurant car to get some dinner. I thought I was so grown-up.' From 26 August, Muriel was again on holiday, this time in Scarborough with her mother and some family friends:

> The weather was wonderful – I got sunburnt on my back and said I'd never do so again – I couldn't lie on it for ages. Sunday 3 September, we go to church and are sent home by the vicar. At the B&B, we stand with other visitors and listen to the radio in the basement. I shall never forget the awful voice of Mr Chamberlain 'We are at war with Germany'. We children had heard the talk and practised going into the air-raid shelter built in the school grounds at Waterloo Park School for Girls, but it didn't mean anything. No trains to get us home for several days. I remember getting off the train with Mother at Seaforth Station and seeing barrage balloons in the sky – silver in the sunshine.

The war which had just been 'grown-up talk' to Muriel was suddenly real. Her brother, Robert, ten years older than Muriel, who was away at his annual two-week camp with the Auxiliary RAF at the time, did not come home for six weeks and, even then, he was only on leave before going away for six years.

There were small changes in the routine of the year's events as well as the bigger ones. Muriel remembers:

> Coming up to Christmas – in previous years Father had always taken me into Liverpool to buy his Christmas presents, but in 1939, he took me to Southport, there having already been several raids on Liverpool. We had hardly got home, when the sirens went and Mum and I went to shelter under the stairs – Dad was out the back watching the bombs and being called to 'Come in!' by us. In each lull, we had to dash into the kitchen for some food and a drink of tea.
>
> Dad had strengthened the hall sides under the stairs with steel plates, which looked pretty awful but saved our lives on the night of the 2 May 1941, when a land-mine dropped. The blast killed all the people in the corner house who had got fed up in the shelter and were all in the kitchen. I had been asleep when it happened and when we couldn't get the door open, I was crying and Mum was telling me we would soon be out. All this time my father and his brother were in the workshop putting out incendiary bombs; in a while Dad came calling for us and

freeing the door. There was a Canadian soldier with him from Seaforth Barracks and he said 'Looks like your house has gone, Ma'am!'

Some children were well aware that their homes were in a vulnerable position. Albert Lewis was eight years old when the war began and lived in Bullens Terrace in Bootle. His home backed onto the railway embankment on the land side of the Marsh Lane/Strand Road railway station and was not very far from the important Bootle Docks. Albert remembers:

> A bomb fell in between the two road (over rail) bridges at this station (gap of fifteen feet!) and left a deep crater… all the houses on our side of the street had cellars and the Local Authority reinforced every one of these cellars, one of which was ours, with heavy corrugated iron roofs, sixteen steel eight foot long tubes each mounted in two foot square of concrete and an escape hatch (brick wall about three foot high with six inch concrete roof with an open end, located in what was the small front garden). Part of the cellar wall of every house was knocked down and replaced with a single brick wall which, in an emergency, would create a means of escape to any house further along our side of the road… In due course both my sister and brother joined the Armed Forces, leaving me as the youngest of the family. This being the case, on hearing air raid sirens, it was my job to run up our rather long lobby to immediately open the front door so that neighbours could come in and take cover in our specially reinforced cellar. After some of the heaviest raids, the sky was a complete circle of fire and fireglow. I witnessed the burning, over a period of three days, of Marsh Lane Station; our house was immediately behind it.

Marjorie Greenwood was nearly nine years old in September 1939, a pupil at St George's School, Everton, and she, too, lived in an exposed and dangerous area:

> Our school was next to St. George's church, which was sited at the highest point in Liverpool. From there, no matter which way you looked, it was all downhill. I lived at 29, Havelock Street with my father, mother and baby brother. Around there, they were all terraced houses; some had steps up to the door; some even had little patches of garden at the front. We were in one of the smaller ones, with neither.

Although, initially, Marjorie was evacuated to Whitchurch, it was for a very short time in the autumn of 1939:

Marsh Lane Station burned for three days.

I stayed with a family in rooms above a bakery. My recollection of staying there, were the huge pots which held jam and honey always with wasps buzzing around. I came home because there was illness in that family and they couldn't cope with extra children.

Marjorie's memories of the air-raid shelters and gas masks that were an integral part of Liverpool life at that time are much more vivid and comprehensive than those of Whitchurch:

I went back to my old school, which was still standing, although you never knew whether it would still be there the next day. Every day at four o'clock, we would come home and get changed into a one-piece suit called a siren suit, which would keep us warm if we ended in the shelters all night. The air raid sirens went off most days and, when they did, we would run up the street to Albion Street to the underground shelter, my mother carrying Tom, my brother, wrapped in a shawl. Most often, we stayed there all night, so there were bunks alongside the walls for us to sleep on. We were glad to hear the All-clear siren, which was a long continuous wailing sound; then the ARP men would come and tell us we could go home. They wore tin helmets with ARP painted on in big, white letters. Everybody carried their gas mask wherever they went. Even babies had a box about two feet long and the baby lay in it. It had a pipe attached which you pumped yourself. Some younger children had a Mickey Mouse gas mask. Often we would come home to find the windows blown in and soot everywhere and, one day, three houses had been flattened from a direct hit. The Fever Hospital adjoined Havelock Street and most nights, the nurses carried the children from there to the Hospital Shelter. Jerry always sent down flares first to light up the target area. Often it seemed like they were aiming at the Children's Hospital, which was a big building. From our house, I could see the nurses lifting the children out of bed and wrapping them in shawls ready for the long night ahead in the shelter. Most of the children were suffering from either Scarlet Fever or Diphtheria.

Marjorie's father worked with the shire horses, used by carters to take goods to the docks. She especially remembers one dramatic incident, 'On one occasion, when we didn't have time to get to the underground shelter, we stayed in our own Morrison shelter, which was in our kitchen.'

The Morrison shelter had been introduced by Ellen Wilkinson, a member of the Churchill's coalition government and the Home Office team led by Herbert Morrison. The shelters were made of very heavy steel and could be used as a table. One of the wire sides lifted up so that people could crawl inside. They were large, providing sleeping space for two or three people, and this meant that they could be space-consuming in a small room. However, they did mean that people did not need to go outside into the cold and damp. Marjorie continues:

At this particular time, my father was at home with us. Usually, he was at work with the horses. The All-clear had gone. It was early morning and Father had made him and Mother a cup of tea. I remember vividly the brown round-bellied teapot. There was an almighty bang. The windows came in and the soot came down the chimney. Father was stood there with just the teapot handle in his hand – no teapot. When we dared to look out, there was a great crater in the street, in which lay an unexploded bomb delivered by Jerry. While the bomb was in the crater, we moved to my Grandmother's house in Cranmer Street. Her back door led into a stable-yard where all the Shire horses lived. There were a lot of horses; some-times only one horse was used to a cart; other times a team of two. While we were staying there, Jerry sent down incendiary bombs which set alight all the stables. I remember a chap coming and telling us not to come out, but, of course, I peeped and saw the men trying to control the horses and steer them out of harm's way up towards Stanley Road. The walls of the house felt hot to the touch. The house became unsafe, although an iron girder was put right through to support it. Eventually, we moved to Aunt Amy's in Lauriston Road, off Queens Drive, Walton. Aunt Amy had an Anderson shelter in the garden; you were only able to have one, if you had a garden. Some tinned food and other things were stored in there for emergencies.

Al Forster was also very young when the war began. He was born in 1938 and his brother, Graham, was two years younger and they lived in Oxton, Wirral. Probably because it was such a dramatic sight, despite their youth, one event made a lasting impression:

We remember to this day, and reminded on a recent visit to Liverpool, seeing a painting of the incident, the Liver Building framed by the flames after bombs fell behind and the whole sky lit up. We had an Anderson shelter at the bottom of the tiny garden. An outside toilet next to it, then a rabbit hutch, then a shed full of tools and bikes etc. and a tiny vegetable patch as well. But we were so rushed, watching, that we had no time to reach the shelter and had to go under the stairs, a cupboard, with a door and a drop-down; as children we were able to hide even further down. And when it was all over, our mum called us to come up, but we kept really quiet and she could not find us. A joke in the midst of all this mayhem!

William (Bill) Backshall was born in 1926 in Litherland into a large and happy family and lived in:

A tiny terrace house – our little street was a cul-de-sac at the end of another dead-end road, with both railway and canal preventing any through traffic, and this geography turned the area into a safe, happy community, where strangers, other than tradesman, and major troubles seldom appeared. Coupled with my family background, this gave me an early sense of security.

Later, as he and his eight brothers and sisters grew bigger, the family moved from Ken Street to a larger house in Marsh Lane, opposite the gasworks, with some land behind it, where Bill's father built a makeshift pigeon loft, with, 'Timber nailed haphazardly together, sections propped up and wedged with bricks, leather tongues cut out of old shoes and boots and used as hinges on doors.' Into Bill's happy world came the shadow of war:

Our first air raid shelter was built with great cunning under the wooden pigeon loft, this flimsy structure alongside the railway fencing. The loft was now defended against the might of the Luftwaffe by packing a row of sandbags round it, giving us a wonderful feeling of security. In reality, a strong breeze or a heavy sneeze could have collapsed the whole thing like the proverbial pack of cards. It became obvious that it was too far from the house to be practical, so a more business-like one was dug on the near lawn with the benefits of heating and lighting. An added bonus was that we didn't have to mow the lawn as frequently. Sadly, at first, it became water-logged, but, once this problem was overcome, it gave great service against falling bombs, shrapnel and other nasties falling in the night.

Joan Gillett lived in Diana Street in the shadow of Everton football ground. She was born in 1938 into a close family and community:

My paternal grandparents and single aunts lived in 19, Diana Street, which had a large cellar and served a shelter during the bombing raids. The cellar was big enough to accommodate a few neighbouring families so it was quite a social gathering.

Joan's father worked for the Dunlop Rubber Company in Rice Lane. After the Fall of Singapore in February 1942, Joan's father was called up: 'My earliest vivid memory is of my Dad going off to war with his suitcase. I remember waving him off at the front door holding my Mum's hand and feeling sad.' Joan's mother, already expecting another child, must have been sad, too. But the close neighbourhood community continued to be an important part of life:

> My next memory is of 12 November 1942, the day my sister, Anne, was born. The baby was due to be born at home because an ambulance could not be guaranteed to take Mum to Oxford Street Hospital. In the event, a nursing sister came from Oxford Street for the birth and had to walk back to the hospital at 3am in the blackout armed with a torch! The nurse was assisted by one of my aunts. I was sent across to 19, Diana Street, to stay with my grandparents for the night. Next morning, the lady who delivered the newspapers told me I had a baby sister. I was thrilled to get home and see Mum and Anne. To my great joy, my Dad came home on a forty-eight hour compassionate leave pass!

Peter Robinson started school at Mosspits Lane, Wavertree; he was four and a half years old and the war had just started. He comments:

> To us in those early days, we knew nothing else. Brick air raid shelters being built in our playgrounds; helping to 'tape up' all the glass windows at school and at home. I used to dread the gas-mask exercises when all us poor kids had to go through smoke-filled shelters to prepare us in the event of a gas attack. There were Anti-Aircraft guns in a main street close by and I remember their blast broke a few windows. We were issued with ear-plugs as the noise was terrible and the house shook.

Children were often fascinated by enemy action, perhaps only recognising its spectacular aspects, and not really comprehending the danger. Terry Grayson, only a year old when war began, lived in Tilston Road, behind the Crown Hotel. Nevertheless he remembers:

> … being taken out to a backyard shelter which was always half-full of water, lying on a type of built-in bed and pulling back the black-out curtain (across the doorway) to watch the searchlights trying to find the German Planes and the noise of the big guns going off.

Terry was only seven when the war ended.

One of the children who looked forward to an air raid, Jim Greer, lived in Wilbraham Street, off Scotland Road, and was only four when the war began:

> Our house had a cellar, converted to an air raid shelter with corrugated sheets and steel supports. It also had a blast wall. When we heard the sirens, we'd go down to the cellar, and the lady who had the sweet shop next door would come into our cellar and bring sweets; hence, as children, and sweets were rationed, we looked forward to the air raids.

Many people, adults and children alike, felt safer in their own homes than in the public shelters, which were dark, often damp, and usually dirty. Ronald Molyneux was nine years old in 1939 and lived in Eton Street in Walton. He says:

> We had shelters built in our street, but no-one used them, only adults for a kiss and a cuddle. We had our cellar reinforced by my uncle and sat there as the bombs dropped. One night, the bombers tried to bomb the railway line a few streets away; they blew up houses a few streets from us and

A public
air-raid shelter
– these were not
universally popular.

Arnot Street school was used as a treatment centre – dead and dying – my aunt being one of the injured. Of course, we were kept away. I recall our house almost being lifted from its foundations, my Grandad still in bed; as he went through the Boer War and the First World War, he was not going to be moved. Big coping stones came through the ceiling, but he remained put.

Three-year-old Elva Barooah, née Kelley, and her mother were evacuated to Hoscar in 1939, and Elva's older sister had been evacuated to Skelmersdale. But they were all home again in Aintree after a short period of time. Elva's memories of the street shelter are more pleasant than those of Ronald Molyneux, but then, she was six years younger than him:

Of course, serious bombing started soon after we returned home. My sister and I slept quite happily under the stairs on a mattress – we drew spiders on the whitewashed wall; they were there years later. Later, shelters were built in the road. I remember being woken up and put into a very cosy hooded siren suit and carried to the shelter. I was excited at seeing the 'fireworks' in the sky. At first, we slept on a mattress, later, bunks were provided. I loved sleeping in the shelters as all the neighbours sat round talking and it seemed so friendly and convivial. I think, but I am not sure, that they all took turns in going out to make tea for everyone.

Joan McMurtry's father was in the Merchant Navy and her young brother was not born until 1942. At the beginning of the war, she was only a year old and her mother felt more secure in her own home:

Our street had its own air-raid shelter, but my mother always preferred to stay in her own house. She found the sense of alarm in the shelter worse than coping on her own. Dad, therefore, put a huge tree-trunk under the stairs for support and made a comfortable nook there. When the sirens went she would go under there with me and her special box - George VI Coronation biscuit tin – which had marriage and birth certificates and insurance policies in. On one occasion, she was sitting there, there was a fizz and an incendiary bomb came through the ceiling. Without picking up the box, she ran out with me into the street. Fortunately, Fire Watch men were soon there and dealt with the bomb. For years after, we had that mark on the ceiling.

David Buckley was eight in 1939 and lived in a flat above Irwin's grocery shop in North Hill Street. David's mother decided that her family would stay together in Liverpool. David remembers:

You would hear the sirens go, then shortly after, you would hear them coming, with the throbbing noise of their engines, then you would hear the bombs dropping. We all used to sit under the stairs, which everyone said was the safest place in the house. But, if the bombing got really bad, the Manager of Irwin's had given the key of the shop to my Mum and we would go down to the cellar, that is, everyone except my Dad. Dad had only one leg after losing the other in the First World War; he could not manage the cellar stairs so used to stay upstairs in the house in the dark, because you could not have a light because of the black-out.

David remembers the evidence of the conflict that was raging over Liverpool all around the area in which he lived:

One of the most frightening things I ever heard was in the May Blitz; we were sitting on the stairs with the door open when we heard the flapping of a land-mine parachute floating down. We just waited and there was an almighty explosion. The next morning, we found out that it had landed in Coletart Street and flattened the whole street. Another night, after a raid, there was a knock at the door and some army personnel told us that there was a time-bomb in a crater at the corner of Maud Street and Merlin Street and that the army disposal squad were defusing it and that we did not have to move, but should stay indoors. In Princes Park, there was a barrage balloon situated on the field opposite Ullet Road. There were rocket guns adjacent to the Needle in Sefton Park and where I lived in North Hill Street, when a raid started, a mobile gun used to come and park directly outside our house; when it started firing, it made a terrific noise. There were brick air raid shelters, built in the middle of the streets, but I don't think many people used them. There were also brick-built Emergency Water Supply (EWS) tanks for use by the Auxiliary Fire Service (AFS). The day after raids, people used to walk about in a daze, because they had been awakened from sleep and then, a few hours later, when the All-Clear had sounded, it was nearly time to get up and go to work or school.

Sometimes familiar places disappeared completely. David recalls:

I belonged to the choir in St Catherine's church in Abercromby Square. When I went for choir practice, I found that the church had been hit by an oil bomb and there was nothing left of it. After a while, Canon Shields, whose church it was, made a church in the small hall at the back of the church and everyone pitched in with different things. One of the teachers made a new cross and lectern.

Conditions in the air-raid shelters were far from comfortable in many cases. And the warning sirens went off at any time. Thomas Eric Wells, born in 1932 and known as Eric to distinguish him from his father, also Thomas, remembers going to a public shelter:

Most of our neighbours went to the underground shelter in Greenbank Park; I cannot recall electric lighting in the shelter, just candles. We used to make our way to the shelter when we had eaten our tea, but one particular night, my father decided that I needed a bath, and whilst I was in the bath, the sirens sounded. I remember my father dashing up to the bathroom, getting me quickly out of the bath and wrapping me in a large towel and running over to the shelter in the park. Sometime after this my father decided to construct a shelter in the house under the stairs; our next-door neighbours agreed to do the same thing, so an opening was made in the party wall of the property, the floor was removed and we stepped down into the space below the floor, enough room for about eight people; two people from over the road joined us each night. It was around this time that a couple of bombs fell about three or four hundred yards away and partially destroyed some houses in Elm Bank Road, and also blew the backs out of a couple of houses in Nicander Road. Our house seemed to rock with the explosions.

Despite his father's efforts to avoid the trips to the public shelter, because of the damp nights in the shelter, Eric's mother caught pneumonia, then pleurisy, and sadly, she died. Eric then lived throughout most of the war with his grandparents at Huyton Quarry, which was then a much more rural area.

Austin Gahan's father attempted to install drainage for their Anderson shelter. Austin was eight years old in 1939 and lived in Norris Green. He recalls:

We dug our air raid shelter (Anderson) which was sunk into the ground. My Dad put in wooden floors and four bunks. He installed a sump to collect water. It was my job to empty it. We put sods of grass on top. We had to use our shelter nearly every night.

Sometimes, parents had to make difficult decisions about their children's welfare. Brian Hill was only five years old when the war began and lived in Clubmoor:

We had an Anderson shelter in the back garden and spent most nights there. The exception was when I had chickenpox and my mother brought a bed downstairs so that I could sleep in the only warm room in the house, heated by a coal fire.

It must have been difficult enough to take a healthy child out of a warm bed and into the outdoor shelter, but the choice must have been agonising when a child was sick. Brian continues:

One night, during an air raid, a bomb fell nearby and our house suffered damage. Plaster fell from the ceiling and some fragments went into the eye of my sister, who was sharing the bed. She cried out 'I'm blind, I'm blind!' but, thankfully, there was no harm done.

Brian lived near a railway bridge on the Cheshire lines, which survived the war, and is now part of the Trans-Pennine Trail:

On one occasion, during an afternoon raid, we were in the shelter and heard the distinctive noise of a German bomber. Being curious, we stood in the garden watching it and heard the whistling noise of a bomb being dropped. We dived back into the shelter – another bomb aimed at the bridge! We were convinced, though, that the pilot had seen us and had aimed the bomb at us! Vivid memories on a young mind, yet I never remember being afraid!

A back yard shelter saved the lives of Beryl Redfern, aged seven in 1939, and her family, whose house was badly damaged:

We lived in Seaforth, so were right in the middle of the May Blitz. We were in the shelter in the back yard – I remember very clearly running through what was left of the house. The furniture was covered in glass – it had gone right through everything. Mum had made a jelly for our tea and the plate was still on top. There was a picture of me hanging on the wall – I still have that picture. My sister, who is three years younger than me, was in a push chair and we ran through the streets after the 'All Clear' to my Grannies' who lived even nearer the Docks. The sky was red from the fires.

Gas masks were one of the things about wartime that no one could ignore or avoid. Elva Barooah, who lived in Aintree and was three years old in 1939, remembers that 'war was just normal living to me... I don't think I had any fears at all about bombing or any aspect of the war other than the gas mask.' Everyone was issued with a gas mask and they were supposed to carry them at all times. Children understood this necessity and were accustomed to doing as they were told, but many children, like Elva, disliked them intensely. We know now that there were no gas attacks, but in 1939, such attacks on the civilian population seemed a real and horrific possibility. The government was aware of the dreadful consequences of gas in the First World War and was anxious to offer people as much protection as possible. Older children were often involved in the distribution of gas masks, either like Reg Cox, who helped his father, an Air Raid Warden, to deliver gas masks to the houses in local streets or in an official capacity. My cousin, Brenda Bryce, née Wright, born in 1930, lived in Peveril Street, off Breeze Hill, and she remembers that gas masks for these streets were delivered by the local Boy Scouts.

Elva's early memories of schooldays are dominated by her worries about her gas mask:

I went to the local elementary school in Rice Lane until I was eight, and the only aspect of the war that intruded was the gas mask inspection. This happened every week. A woman came round and tested each one – I think she put a piece of paper at the bottom to see if we could inhale. I was terrified – not of the fear of being gassed – but I just felt when I had it on I couldn't breathe and thought if I had to wear it for any length of time, I would choke to death.

David Ferguson started school and remembers being issued, because he was so young, with:

... a Mickey Mouse gas mask which I only wore to see how to put it on and it remained in its box for the rest of the war, as, fortunately, there were no gas attacks. Also at school, we had air raid drills to make sure we knew what to do if the sirens went off.

Evelyn Davies, née Courtman, was ten in 1939 and describes her gas mask as an ever-present nuisance for a happy and carefree little girl, rather than a frightening omen of the potential horrors of war:

Our gas masks were issued and fitted at school by helpers who showed us what to do if need be. I remember trying mine on only once, and it smelled of rubber. It was in a cardboard container which my mother changed for a more substantial black tin canister with a cord, which eventually ended up with many dents because of the careless way I treated it. Swinging it round and round or dropping it many times. It was an encumbrance that had to be carried at all times! You were even sent home from school to get it, if you had forgotten to bring it with you.

James Middleton remembers the dramatic effects of a practice gas attack:

One day, we were told that a simulated gas attack was going to take place in our neighbourhood, using real gas, and our teacher stressed that we must not forget to take our gas masks to school. This we did, and spent the whole day in fear and trepidation waiting for this frightening thing to happen, but nothing did! However, when we went home from school, Mum told us that when she had gone down to our local shops, the fumes of the tear gas were still hanging around and many of the assistants had streaming eyes, so some gas bombs must have been set off.

Chapter Two

The 'yo-yo children'

Mass evacuation of school-age children is already a well-documented aspect of the children's experience of the Second World War and, although many children were not included in this group, it does form part of a full picture. There were also other forms of government sponsored evacuation for some groups. These included the blind and disabled, pregnant women and mothers with babies or pre-school-age children.

However, many of these very young children and babies were not evacuated because their mothers did not want to spend the war as 'lodgers' in other people's homes. Nor did they want to leave their homes empty and vulnerable, if their husbands were already away in the Services. Women often felt the need to 'keep the home fires burning'. If a husband serving in the Forces was able to get some leave, he wanted to see his wife in the privacy of their own home and not in the unfamiliar and inhibited surroundings of a strange house in a strange area of the country. Women whose husbands were in reserved occupations, those whose work and skills were vital to the war effort, wanted to be at home to care for their comfort. Cooking, washing, getting clothes dry, cleaning and ironing were much more time consuming in the 1930s and 1940s and, as the war progressed, queuing for food took hours. Men were unaccustomed to these tasks and there was no expectation that they should learn new skills now, or the time or opportunity to do so, when many in these vital occupations were working long hours of compulsory overtime. So many women with babies and very young infants chose not to be evacuated. And those women who had been evacuated with babies or very young children often came home again, when they saw how difficult it was for husbands to cope with a day's work and housekeeping, often with little sleep after nights in the air-raid shelters.

Eileen Sweeney's memory of evacuation to Southport illustrates one of the reasons why women with very young children, who could have been evacuated with them, often chose to stay at home or to return home. Eileen says:

I was born in Bootle in 1934. There was Mum and Dad, a sister eighteen months older than me, and my baby brother, Brian, who was born in 1939. He was just six months old when we, Mum, sister, Brian and myself, were evacuated to Park Road, Southport, to a Dr Cairns and his wife. They had a big house with a maid and gardener. My Dad stayed at home looking after things. One weekend, he came to visit and asked if he could stay for the weekend to spend some time with his family; he was told it was not allowed. Dad was quite upset and said if he couldn't stay, we would all have to leave. Dr Cairns said he was a silly man, as all the money he got for looking after us was going to be given to us when the war was over. We were dressed and got a bus back to Bootle. Years later, my Dad told us that we would all have been killed if we had stayed in Dr Cairns' house as it had a direct hit from a bomb and they were all killed – one of the few bombs dropped on Southport.

The difficulties of satisfying the needs of all the members of a family inevitably led to different experiences between siblings, sometimes casting a long shadow. One anonymous family consisted of three sisters. Their father was away in the Services and their mother was doing shift work in munitions. The twelve-year-old eldest sister was kept at home to care for the pre-school-age sister when the mother was at work on night shifts. The eight-year-old middle sister was evacuated with the school. The oldest child remembers sitting, terrified, in the air raid shelter holding her baby sister and thinking that no-one cared whether she was bombed. The home-sick middle sister remembers wondering why she had been sent away while everyone else stayed at home. The youngest sister, blamed by nobody and on good terms with both sisters is, nevertheless, aware that there are tensions between her two sisters because of those days when each felt that the other had been more cared for than she had been.

There were physical dangers for those children who stayed at home, but if their immediate families were not killed or injured in the bombing, they did not suffer the emotional trauma experienced by those children whose experiences of evacuation were unhappy. The difficulties of deciding whether children should 'go or stay' are illustrated by Peggy Rider's memory. Peggy was seven when the war began and lived in Old Swan:

School was disbanded and the children were meeting (to be evacuated) in the school playground. My mother and I went as far as the playground, but then decided to go home while all the other children were evacuated.

Barbara Yorke, née Norton, remembers being evacuated with her school:

At the outbreak of war, the all-girls school that I attended, Calder High School, was evacuated to Wrexham. I can remember having a luggage label with my name on it, tied to the button-hole of my school blazer. Then we went to Birkenhead for the train to North Wales. It was a long day. Eventually, a family who had a car, and one son aged about ten, took myself and an older girl. I can remember being asked my surname and not being familiar with the expression 'surname' left it to the teacher to read my label. We really did have to have our gas-masks in cardboard boxes with us all the time. One night, feeling very home-sick, I remembered my gas-mask contained an 'emergency' bar of chocolate. I couldn't resist, so ate it with no thought of how I would replace it. After about a month, I went home, only to return about a month after that to go to another family, who had taken in my cousin, whose family I lived with in Liverpool. Our host had two younger girls and I remember sleeping on a camp-bed.

We went to school for half-days, as we were sharing the school building with local children. After returning for Christmas, it was decided that, as our school buildings at Calder High, were, supposedly, out of the danger-zone for bombing, we could all stay at home. Any child who lived nearer to the city centre would be evacuated to stay with a school-fellow who lived in a safe area. Air raid shelters were built in the school grounds, which I remember well. I stayed at Calder High until 1948, when I went to do teacher-training at Colquitt Street Domestic Science College. This had been badly bombed and, even then, we had to walk round mounds of rubble going from one part of the college to another.

Enid Johnston tells of an act of kindness that led to a long-standing friendship:

> On 29th October 1940, there was a mine which landed in the largest gas-holder at Garston
> Gasworks. This was at 3am and so fortunate that it did not go off. The man in charge noticed
> that the holder was rapidly going down and had the presence of mind to turn off the supplies.
> The man who dismantled the mine was Lieutenant Newgass and for this act of bravery he
> was awarded the Victoria Cross. My personal memory of this is that because all the people
> round the Gasworks had to be evacuated, lots of people had nowhere to go and my mother,
> out shopping, came across two complete strangers looking for somewhere to stay, and she
> invited them to stay with us for the duration of the evacuation. Although I was quite young
> then, I well remember Mr and Mrs Barber staying with us, and they became good friends of
> my family for many, many years after.

In fact, Lieutenant Harold Reginald Newgass of the Royal Naval Volunteer Reserve is listed
as having received the George Cross for his courage on 4 March 1941. The Victoria Cross is
awarded for valour in the face of the enemy, while the George Cross is for valour in other
circumstances. It must be deemed that bomb disposal, while the direct result of enemy action,
is not in the face of the enemy. Nevertheless, it is a measure of the impression that this man's
courage made, and the gratitude felt by the community to him, that a little girl of six years
old should remember his name more than sixty years later. Other small acts of kindness and
neighbourliness are remembered by Sonia Part, who was seven in 1939 and lived in Fazakerley:

> We were invited by neighbours to share their shelter at night. One night, when we were in the
> shelter, the air raid warden came, saying 'You've got to get out, there's a time-bomb next door.
> The houses over the road had collapsed.' We had to run to our house; our front door had been
> blown off and all the windows blown out. We had to grab a few things and go to the church
> hall in Barlows Lane until they dealt with the unexploded bomb. One little thing that hap-
> pened that night was my best friend's little kitten could not be found, so she and I came back
> to the street. It was barricaded by soldiers who wouldn't let us through, of course. However, we
> and the soldiers started calling the little cat and it came strolling up the street. My friend picked
> it up to love it. But we couldn't take it where we were, so we went round the houses in Barlows
> Lane asking if someone would mind it. A very kind lady did so.

Unlike Sonia's story, very few of the childhood memories include any mention of family
pets. People were discouraged from keeping pets, because of the difficulties of feeding
them. However, Joan Tisdale, eleven in 1939, remembers her grandad's pigeons:

> My Grandad kept pigeons and he used to let me see them and feed them, but I was very upset
> when he told me that they had to go away and do Secret Service work and I may not see
> them again.

Some friendships were made at this time of adversity that have lasted ever since. Elizabeth
Charles remains close to a fellow evacuee:

> I always remember waiting on the platform of Lime Street Station with hundreds of chil-
> dren… for trains to take us to our destination; we all carried the little boxes containing our gas
> masks. I was sent to a little remote farm with two other children from my school… they were
> two sisters and even now one of them lives by me and we have been friends all these years.

Elizabeth was evacuated from Walton in 1940, aged seven.

Pat Lawrenson was only four years old when the war began and, because she was under school age, she was evacuated from Walton with her mother and sister to Burscough. Pat says:

> My dad stayed at home to go to work. He worked in Taylor's bakery in Buchanan Road, Walton. My dad was forty-two at the beginning of the war, so wasn't called up for the Forces. He was in the First World War, aged seventeen… My sister was in Fazakerley Open-air School for a while. My mum and I didn't stay long in Burscough. A few months, I think. When we were all back home, we used to go under the stairs in the air raids. We only went in the shelters in the street a couple of times. Two of my aunties were there with their babies. My brother was born in 1942.

Pat's family, like many others, seem to have drawn comfort from being together. There were the practical difficulties for husbands left to cope at home and many women did not like sharing a stranger's home. Pat's mother had the company and support of female relatives at home, and the logistics of getting a number of young children into the public shelter probably explains why Pat's mother and aunts, like many other people, preferred the under-stairs space, which was warm and private, if cramped. As the war progressed, people began to lose faith in the public shelters, as some of them received direct hits and were obliterated. Many people believed that the under-stairs space against the load-bearing walls of their houses offered a better protection.

Eileen Doyle, who lived in Dryden Street, Bootle, at the beginning of the war, wrote, 'There were five of us, three girls and two boys.' Eileen and her sisters and brothers went to Ireland to live with her father's sister. Eileen says, 'I think that my Dad thought it would only last about six months. We left from Gladstone Docks at 10p.m. on 3 September 1939. We stayed about nine months, then we came home.' Eileen clearly sees this stay with family as quite different from going to strangers, as she writes, 'I was one of those children who didn't get evacuated, my Mum wouldn't let us.' There is no doubt that children who went to stay with family or to live with friends experienced less emotional upset than those involved in mass evacuation to strangers, even those children who were fortunate enough to find themselves in comfortable and caring foster homes.

When Eileen did come home, the family had an Anderson shelter in the back yard, but she remembers that:

> We all went in the under the stairs cupboard and when the raids got very bad we went in the shelter… a land-mine landed on the house next door, killing one person. Our house was very badly damaged. We lost everything, nothing was saved. Women and children had to go to Bootle Town Hall… they took us to St Helens to a church hall; it was full… we all had to sleep on the floor.

When Eileen's father, who worked on the docks, came out to see them:

> … he went to the pub… and asked the local men if they knew anyone to give us a couple of rooms. One man took in my Mum and three children and another took my eldest sister and me home with him… they had a spare bedroom as their sons were in the Army. It wasn't far from my Mum's place. So we were lucky to find some kind people to take us in.

Reg Cox experienced both types of evacuation. In late 1939, at ten years old:

> I went to stay with my Uncle Jack and Aunt May in Craven Arms in Shropshire… it was an idyllic time for me, a young city lad, let loose in the country, all sorts of things I'd not seen

before, hazel nuts, sticklebacks, frogspawn; my aunt and uncle looked after me very well and there were two older cousins, Lilian and Arthur. Lilian made a big fuss of me and Arthur tolerated me. Uncle Jack was the Manager of Stubbs Meeson, a Seed Merchant, and I can remember the excitement of the workmen letting me ride up sitting on a sack of grain on the hoist to the top of the building. I don't think Health and Safety would be too happy about that now!

In 1940, Reg was evacuated again through the official programme of evacuation to Greenfield, near Holywell, in North Wales. Reg points out that:

Greenfield sounds like another idyll, but… it was a small industrial town on the River Dee with a huge Cortaulds factory and a paper mill. I remember seeing the red glow in the sky over the Wirral, as a result of the first air raids on Liverpool, but then there was a gap, nothing much happened. My parents came to see me as often as they could, but it was a long journey on trains. I was getting homesick, I suppose, and as there was not much going on in Liverpool, my parents brought me home, just in time for the May Blitz in 1941.

The initial wave of mass evacuation had its own impetus, but children who missed this wave, for any reason, often stayed at home throughout the war. The period of inaction at the end of 1939 and the return of many of the first evacuees meant that parents, who may not have wanted to let their children go away, felt less pressure to do so. For instance, Lawrence Whittaker, four in 1939 and living near Scotland Road, missed being evacuated because he had chickenpox. Despite still being very young, he has 'very clear memories of the May Blitz of 1941' and remembers 'being bombed out twice' and 'streets with the houses ablaze from the bombing'.

Some children were not evacuated in 1939, but later events changed their parents' minds. Arthur Williams says:

I was nine years of age when the war started; being evacuated was suggested to all parents, but my parents declined… In 1941, it was in the May Blitz. We had spent the night in the air-raid shelter and when the all-clear sounded, we went back to our house but there wasn't a roof or windows. They had all blown out, because a quarter of a mile from us, at Clubmoor, an ammunition train had a direct hit and it devastated a lot of houses. That was the last straw…the family had had enough. The police came round and the children were rounded up and assembled at the Pierhead with our gas masks and little cases and were evacuated to Colomendy for two years. Our parents were crying, not knowing when they would see us again or even if! We were actually allowed to see our parents once a month.

Colomendy Camp in North Wales has been visited by more than 350,000 schoolchildren on holiday, most coming from Liverpool but with some international camps. However, it was built originally in 1939 by the National Camps Corporation, not as a holiday centre but as a wartime refuge for Liverpool schoolchildren. The first children to arrive in 1940 were from the Dingle area, a dockland district in great danger from enemy bombing, which was rendered more dangerous by the existence of a local oil storage depot. Conditions were fairly basic. The children slept in dormitories, each with twenty-nine beds. There were problems because the children came from all sorts of backgrounds and close living conditions meant that head lice, scabies and other infections were easily transmitted. Some children enjoyed the freedom and friendships and stayed at Colomendy for the whole of the war, but shy children or children missing their families were less settled.

Austin Gahan, from Norris Green, and his sister were there for a short time, 'My sister and I were evacuated to Colomendy Camp. But, as my sister could not cope with the camp, she was returned to Liverpool and lived with our aunt in West Derby. I do not know how long I was there.' But Austin could not have stayed long at Colomendy because most of his memories are of wartime Liverpool.

Some children were evacuated right at the beginning of the war in September 1939 with their school but were not always welcomed. Ralph Pedersen, four years old, lived in Pitt Street, and went to Hoole in Cheshire from St Peter's RC School in Gilbert Street, with his cousin, Peter, aged six. Ralph says:

> I cannot remember the people who took us in, but we must have been a cultural shock — two small boys from the centre of Liverpool with strange accents and, being so young, not properly trained. They would not allow us to stay in the house during the day, so when my aunt came to visit and found us sitting outside, she immediately took us away. Back to Liverpool and the nightmare of the May Blitz, at least we were back home.

Although still only eleven years old in 1945, Ralph's memories describe wartime in the heart of the city of Liverpool extremely graphically:

> The raids were a nightmare, but they could also be beautiful; the sight of the searchlights scanning across the sky at night; light shining off the barrage balloons and lighting the low clouds, feathers against a midnight-blue sky, looking so close you could almost touch them; the night the Custom House was hit I shall never forget, it was like a night from Dante's Inferno and yet, at the same time, beautiful. In the dark night, the dome of the Custom House glowed like a red ball that seemed like a volcano about to erupt…a ship in dry-dock was hit and exploded, causing tremendous damage… one of the buildings bombed at this time was St Michael's in the City in Pitt Street, but it was not demolished, it stood with its columns and towers of stone, obviously highly dangerous. The army came and used dynamite, while we stood and watched part of our environment disappear. About this time, a barrage balloon had come down and was hanging deflated on the roof of St Vincent's like a grey shroud.

When Ralph was evacuated again, after the May Blitz, this time it was to Northwich with his grandma and other children from his family, he says:

> This time it was more pleasant… we enjoyed the pleasures of the countryside; it was a new world with exciting discoveries. I remember once we found a shed with some baby chicks and never having seen chickens before, we were fascinated and took some of them home and put them in a drawer, but they made a noise and were found and returned to their owner. It was here that I first saw bluebells and I remember standing in the woods in a sea of blue. Perhaps it might be thought sad that a town boy was finding nature at the age of six, but it was an awakening and it was magical!

Nevertheless, he comments about evacuation:

> The only sad times were when my mother came to visit and I thought she was taking me home with her. I would go to the bus stop and climb to the top deck, only to be told to get off the bus as I was staying. It was rejection. Children need stability in their lives, usually it is their mothers, and when it is not there, they can be lonely.

Most mothers were only too well aware of this need; the desire to protect their children pulled them in two directions. They wanted their children to be safe from physical harm, but also wanted them to be happy and secure.

Mothers were torn two ways; this poster shows the official attitude.

Evacuation and separation from parents often placed responsibility for younger siblings, other relatives or friend's children, on the shoulders of children who were themselves very young, confused and homesick and who would in normal circumstances have been living through a still carefree stage of their lives. Yet, it was only natural for a mother to tell a seven or eight-year-old-child to take care of a younger brother, sister or cousin and not to be separated from them.

Patricia Whittington Richardson writes from the USA with her memories. Patricia, only four-and-a-half was evacuated to Wales with her brother, Norman Whittington, aged seven. Norman reassured Patricia that he would not leave her. However, when they arrived in Wales, Patricia says:

> There was a voice on a loudspeaker saying 'Girls to the left; boys to the right' My brother stayed with me, and although several times an adult would try to get him to go with the other boys, he refused. I believe he was the only boy with, it seemed to me, a hundred girls.

This little boy showed great moral courage to stay with his sister as he had promised his parents, in the face of adult disapproval and persuasion, and separation from his own friends.

Norman and Patricia went to a farm in Radnorshire, where conditions were primitive and the elderly brother and sister were strict, the farmhouse 'stark and cold'. The children had to share beds, Patricia with the old lady, Norman with the old man. Patricia continues:

> One day, I was sent to feed the pigs, but upon attempting to open the gate to the sty and, seeing the size of the pigs (they looked like elephants to me) I screamed, dropped the steel bucket containing potato peelings and ran back to the house. I received a scolding and my brother was sent to complete the job. I remember we had to cross a stream to get to school and my brother told me to ride 'piggyback' so I wouldn't get my shoes wet. I was extremely unhappy and unknown to me, my brother wrote on one of the pre-stamped postcards that my parents had given to him 'Pat is crying and wants to come home.' He waited for the postman and persuaded him to mail it. A few days later I was outside sitting with my brother on a haystack when I recognised my father walking along the country road. I ran to him and he repeatedly told the story over the years 'She clung to my trouser leg; there was no way she was letting go!' Apparently, on receiving the postcard, my mother told my father to go and get us 'We'll all go together, if that's to be the case.'

Patricia added:

> Whenever I am in a train station I immediately become tense – it took me years to realise that it was due to that experience – to this day I feel indebted to my brother for taking such good care of me.

Irene Collinson, aged ten in 1939, writes:

> Yes, I was evacuated… with my two younger brothers, Bill and Brian, who was only four
> years old. First to Southport and then to Wales; I was billeted with Brian so I could look
> after him. My other brother, Bill, was with the lady's sister, Aunt Maud. We had Aunt Marge
> and Uncle Jack. I went to the village school in Llandrindod Wells, but I came home before
> the boys because I was fourteen in the July of 1943, and leaving school. Poor boys were sad
> without me.

Frederick Berwick, six in December 1939, had two younger siblings. His father was fighting in Africa and his mother went out to work, so, at home, he had a lot of responsibility
for the younger children. At first, they were not evacuated and Frederick took his turn at
queuing for rations, 'We even queued up for "fades", which were damaged fruit'. He also
went to Solomon Street washing baths, where he would queue and pay for a machine and
wait for his mother to come with the washing.

Later, he went to Holt on the River Dee, North Wales. Unlike some children, who had
more responsibility for younger ones when away from home, for Frederick, this was his
most carefree time:

> There was some relief when I was evacuated. My brother and sister were sent to other fami-
> lies. I was sent to a big house with three other boys from my class. Mrs. Cleary, who was our
> teacher, was housed with us and she would take us on nature rambles, showing us things we
> had never seen before. This was so different from anything we had ever known; fields to play
> in; orchards with fruit to pick and pigs eating the windfalls. We explored everywhere; it was
> an idyllic time. However, it was short-lived, as the lady we were staying with, wrote to my
> mother to say I needed new boots and would she send the money. My mother did not have
> it, so she sent for us.

Many of the Liverpool evacuees came from areas where the population was predom-
inantly Roman Catholic. Concerns were expressed in the *Liverpool Echo* in the early
months of the war regarding the difficulties of Catholic children following their faith
and the anti-Catholic feeling perceived to exist in North Wales, the destination of many
Liverpool children. However, only one of my correspondents has mentioned this as a
negative aspect of their recollections. Before the war, different communities had little
contact and knew very little about each other, so prejudice could exist. But in wartime,
children came into contact with people of different denominations. Indeed, it has been
suggested by a number of people that the ecumenical advances made in Liverpool by
Archbishop Warlock and Bishop David Shepherd were partly possible because many of
the adult generation of the 1980s had come to realise, through evacuation, that there were
good and kind people in all faiths.

Pat Sharkey, née Hill, from Tuebrook, aged ten in 1939, believes that her mother
encountered some anti-Catholic feeling in Mold and made no friends there, but she also
says:

> I was very happy in Mold, a very kind family called Roberts took me. The house was very
> pleasant with a large garden and fields behind it, a farm to obtain milk, woods to pick hazel
> nuts and a river to fish with jam jars.

Victor (Vic) Smith was born in 1934 and was evacuated with Lidderdale Road Infants School:

> We left by train at Sefton Park Station to travel to Flint. A meal was prepared for us in Cortauld's canteen after which we were taken by bus to Bagillt. Although it sounds surprising, I was more excited than terrified at being taken away from my parents at such a young age. It must have been much worse for our parents. My host family, the Edwards, consisted of mother, father, three sisters and a brother, all of the siblings, by then adult, welcomed me so that I quickly felt happily at home. I realised only later how lucky I had been. I stayed with the Edwards until the remaining evacuees had to go home at the end of the war when I was eleven years old. The Mayor of Flint shook our hands and saw us off at the station. I returned to Bagillt many times in the holidays and at weekends and kept in touch with the family until the last daughter, Eluned, died in 1999.

Stanley Lewis, born in July 1926 and living in Birkenhead, was evacuated to Wales in 1939. Because of its proximity to Liverpool, the docks and the existence of the Cammel Laird Shipyard, Birkenhead, although on the Wirral, was never considered to be a safe area. Sadly, Stan died aged forty-seven, but his daughter, Linda Leaworthy, has made available the letters that he wrote from Wales to his parents, Bill and Ada, who treasured them. The letters begin in 1939 and go on until 1941, by which time Stan was fifteen and had left school. As soon as he was old enough, Stan joined the King's Regiment, Liverpool, one of the oldest infantry regiments in the country, having been formed in 1685. Stan rose through the ranks from Private to Captain, serving in India during the period when that country gained its independence. He later joined the police. His letters show that he was whole-hearted in everything he undertook and quickly learnt to 'stand on his own two feet'.

Stan was evacuated first with his older brother, Billy, to Towyn (Tywyn), Merioneth. There was a young sister, Eva, aged about three years old at home. Stan writes on 26 November 1939. His letter is, at first, concerned with chocolate and football, but, as it progresses, it becomes clear that he misses his family and would very much like to see them, although he tries not to ask for the impossible:

> Dear Mum & Dad & Eva,
>
> I hope you are all keeping well, I am keeping fine. We got your parcel on Saturday, the Kit Kat was a fine surprise. I only hope we get some more like it. We got beat on Saturday because we were playing great big boys and not the little ones as we thought but still we only got beat 2-1, not bad was it. I scored but it wasn't counted. I hope you will soon be coming to see us here, if you write and tell us we will be very glad to meet you… The soldiers went home on Friday night at half past twelve, but I think there is a new battery coming soon so we can get our cigarette cards from them. Well, I have got to go to church now, so goodbye.
>
> Love from Stan.

He ends his letter with forty-six kisses, but these are formed into a large capital EVA, presumably to indicate that this is for his little sister's benefit and not because he is feeling sentimental!

By April 1940, Billy has returned home because he has reached school-leaving age, and Stan is writing:

> I hope you are all well and safe at home. There is nothing certain about us going to Aberdovey, so don't get worrying about us moving… If we move to Aberdovey, I am coming home.

By this time, Stan is nearly fourteen and has a part-time job; he writes home for advice:

> You know Mr Evans, the man I work for, well, this week the two assistants left him to join the ATS and there is only one left and me. Mr Evans said he would like me to work for him behind the counter, but he is only paying 15/- a week & this is if I leave school. I don't think it's worth it, do you? Because if I pay Mrs Roberts 12/6 as is the billeting allowance, well, that will leave only 2/6 out of 15/- and I can't send you anything for you to pay for clothes. So it's not worth it, is it?

Clearly, one of the problems of growing up away from home for many young people must have been the delay in receiving advice and guidance by post in everyday trivial matters, as well as more important issues, such as whether to leave school or take a particular job, as outlined by Stan Lewis. This is also evident when Stan, who does move to Aberdovey but does not leave school, needs to have a form completed. He writes:

> I am fine here. My billet gets better every day. Thanks for the slippers – they fit fine. I am carrying on my confirmation classes in Aberdovey. The Vicar here has given me a slip which he wants me to fill in, so I am sending it for you to fill in and if you will send it back by this week, it will do me fine.

Some children who had been happy in one foster home found it difficult to settle elsewhere and, often, a child would go home at this stage. Stan's letter show that he had not been keen on a change but that he settled down in Aberdovey. As well as his confirmation classes, he had other interests.

> Tell Dad that I passed my signalling on Friday and that I have only got 3 more tests to pass before I become a second class scout. And also tell him that I am the School Captain of Games and everything else. We are playing Aberdovey School a football match on Wednesday & I am playing Centre Half and Captain. I will let you know the result of the match next Sunday.

Some children were evacuated to a country area, but Aberdovey is a seaside town at the mouth of the River Dovey, and Stan found himself involved in its life-style. He writes:

> During the school holidays, I have been helping to paint Mrs Jones' son's boat and he promised to take me out when it is ready. I was out on the river in a boat with one of the

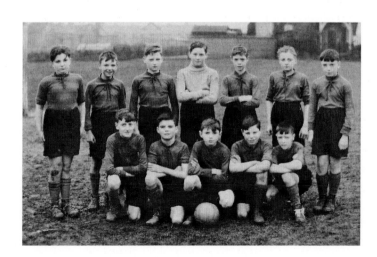

Stan Lewis is the goalkeeper; as an evacuee he played centre-forward.

fishermen the other day and didn't I have some fun. By the time I come home I will be an expert rower.

But there was always the shadow of war. Stan writes:

I hope you are all safe after that last heavy Blitz. Last night I went to the Pictures at Machynlleth to see 'The Great Dictator' – it was very funny but not as funny as I expected. Mrs Jones' son, who is a prisoner-of-war in Germany is fine (so he says) and he has found a friend in the same camp who is from Aberdovey. In your next letter tell me how much damage had been done to Birkenhead and will you tell me if the Children's Hospital has been hit as Mrs Jones has got a niece working there and she doesn't know if the hospital has gone west or not, so will you tell me please. Will you tell Dad that the Scouts have had to be disbanded as the Scoutmaster has been called up. But they tell me it will start again. I hope so.

Terrie McAsey was evacuated, aged seven, with her three brothers, twice. 'We were sent to Colwyn Bay to a Boarding House. The man who owned it was Italian; he disappeared, so we came home.' It is impossible to know whether he was interned or what became of him.
Terrie's family were evacuated for the second time to Aberarth:

… but no-one wanted to take four children. Eventually we were split up, the last children in the Village Hall. I was taken by a Mrs Evans, wife of Captain Evans, as a playmate for her daughter, Jean, the same age as me. We became great friends, but I lost touch with her when I grew up. I was lucky – it was a huge house (to a small child). We had a cook, a maid, everything I could want. Mrs Evans took me to concerts and theatres and gave me my love, continuing all my life, of show business. I was very happy there, but my Dad, when he came home on leave from the Navy, made us all come home. I was the last to do so and it was two years of love and contentment, so I was one of the lucky ones.

Jim Greer was the eleventh of twelve children and the youngest of those to be evacuated. The twelfth child, his sister, Pat, was born in the air-raid shelter in March 1941:

As I was the youngest, my mother instructed my sister, Margaret, that whoever selected her, must take me. I recollect trawling the streets of Bangor in a bus, stopping at houses and people coming on the bus selecting children – my sister was selected and told the person, she would have to take me; this she did and the bus drove away with my two brothers aboard. We were looking for them next day and found them two streets away.

This story illustrates the huge scope for anxiety that existed in the selection process, particularly for older children. Jim's sister, Margaret, must have been relieved when she located her other brothers. However, Jim continues:

We spent about eighteen months in Bangor, my sister and I with a lovely lady, Mrs Williams, who was upset when we eventually went home. But my brothers had a short stay due to a fracas between my mother and the Welsh lady, over her wanting to charge for washing clothes. My mother took my brothers home.

Some people's memories clearly show that the stereotypical view of deprived inner-city children being foisted on healthy-living, rosy-cheeked country folk was often far from the truth. After Eileen Sweeney's family returned from Southport, she and her sister were evacuated, without her mother and baby brother, to Hereford. Eileen remembers:

Our troubles really started then. We didn't get a lot to eat, but I can remember the powdered egg and fried bread. On the way home from school we used to eat the leaves on the trees, which tasted like cheese. We had a long walk to school. Our feet were sore as the shoes we had on were full of holes. When we finally got home, we had to wait in the shed until the woman or her son would come home from work; she worked half-days. She made us get washed in the brook outside the house where the cows came to drink and spend a penny; our heads were full of nits and lice and we had sores on our bodies. We often thought of running away with the gypsies that were in the country lane opposite the house, and continually wrote little letters to our Mum and Dad to please bring us home. It was on a visit from my Mum that she stayed overnight and saw the distressed condition we were in, pillows full of lice and scratching all night. The next morning my Mum got us ready and we came back home. The rest of the war years were not pleasant as we had scabies and were in and out of hospital or going to Balliol Road baths to have our sores painted with some sort of white medication. I have no happy memories of the war, only of those things I will never forget.

Phil Taylor recorded his memories for a school project for his granddaughter. Phil died in 2004, but his wife sent me that project, *Grandad's memories of war*:

I was six years old when war was declared. All our school was evacuated to Bridgenorth. I was with my older sisters, Teresa and Peggy, and older brother, Tom. When we reached Bridgenorth, we went to a school hall and were issued with a brown paper bag with groceries in it for the people where we were going to live. After a long wait, I was taken with my sister Peggy to a house. I remember being very tired and I almost fell asleep on my feet. The lady was very nice and I have good memories of my time there. After a few months, Peggy was fourteen and went home and I went to live with Teresa. I was never home-sick. It was a lovely place and lovely people. We had our own teachers. It was a different life in the country to what we were used to
  After months nothing was happening to Liverpool. It was the period called 'the phoney war'. Then the bombing started and once again all the young children were sent away to the country. This time, my brother, Billy, aged five, came with us. Teresa was now ten and Tommy was eleven. We ended up in Caernarvon, in Wales. This time we all went to different houses. Billy was very upset and after four months, he went home. Then Teresa went home. I stayed for eighteen months and Tommy stayed until he was fourteen. It was a very strange life because Welsh was spoken mostly and we only went to school half days and seemed to spend the other half fighting the Welsh boys. Many children went home because of problems in their billets, as they were called. Some ran away and tried to walk back to Liverpool. When I was nine, I went back to Liverpool and most of the others were back also.

One wonders when 'the Welsh boys' went to school if they were not at school in the half of the school day when the evacuees were free.
  Children's Hour on BBC radio on 13 October 1940, during the Battle of Britain, included a five-minute message broadcast by HRH the Princess Elizabeth to 'the children of the Empire'. In it, she said 'My sister and I feel so much for you as we know what it means to be away from those we love'. This message, although mainly intended for evacuees, would, of course, also have had meaning for all those children whose parents, mainly fathers, were in the Services. And as it was broadcast during *Children's Hour*, it would have been heard by many thousands of children. The words that had been approved for the Princess to broadcast reinforced the message of the *Liverpool Echo*, which had discouraged children from becoming 'doleful'. The fourteen-year-old Princess said 'I can truthfully say to you all that we children at home are full of cheerfulness and courage. We are trying to do all we can to help our gallant airmen, soldiers and sailors and we are trying to bear our own share of the danger and sadness of war.

Chapter Three

Lucky Escapes

Children were, undoubtedly, showing tremendous 'cheerfulness and courage' in the face of all the strange and, sometimes, frightening events of the times in which they were living. The awful possibilities of war were brought home to John Johnson, aged twelve, and his family in 1941, when they had not one, but two narrow escapes from danger:

> My mother had put her name down for a Corporation house in the year I was born, which was 1929; (my parents) very much wanted to move from Carmel Street as it was near town. In 1941, they were offered a house in Suburban Road, Cabbage Hall. Just before deciding to move they got an offer of another Corporation house in West Derby. Luckily enough, they chose to move to the house in West Derby. Why? Well, we moved on a Tuesday in May in the Blitz. That night a large bomb dropped on the house in Carmel Street, and an oil bomb dropped in the front garden of the house in Suburban Road.

John was a Boy Scout messenger during the war years, based at the Mansion House on Queens Drive, which was later to become the local library. He saw some strange sights, such as a bomb hanging in the branches of a tree when the school in Ballantyne Road, Clubmoor was hit. Many years later, John saw the same bomb displayed in the window of the Gas Showroom in Bold Street. The Scouts, as well as 'doing their bit' for the war effort, were determined to continue their other pursuits. John's troop would pile their camping gear onto their handcart and walk to a station on the Liverpool to Ormskirk railway. They would leave the train at Ormskirk and pull the handcart to Tawd Vale Campsite, which still belongs to the Scouts. John Johnson retained his links with scouting, rising to District Commissioner. Many boys over the years should be glad that John and his family missed those two bombs in 1941.

John also recalls:

> In July, I was at the Pier Head landing stage and saw the 'Arandora Star', a ship loaded with German and Italian prisoners-of-war. We called names at them. It sailed later that day; next day, it was torpedoed and sunk by a U-boat.

This must have been on 1 July 1940, when John was eleven years old. The SS *Arandora Star* was a Blue Star luxury cruise liner – one of 'The Luxury Five'. In peacetime, she was a very well-known ship, described as having 'palatial surroundings with a Louis XIV-style dining-room'. She left Liverpool at 4 a.m. on 2 July 1940. The ship was taking German and Italian internees to St John's, Newfoundland. Some of these deportees had lived in this country for many years; some were German Jews and other non-Nazis who had fled from Hitler's regime. Only eighty-six were actually prisoners-of-war. The SS *Arandora Star* was sunk by German *U-47*. There were only 868 survivors of the 1,673 aboard, including officers, crew and the military guard. The sinking of the *Arandora Star* led to protests about the government policy of internment and this was altered. The name *Arandora* was not used by the Blue Star Line again.

Another ship that was torpedoed in 1940 was the SS *City of Benares*. This ship was part of the convoy OB-213 and was used in the overseas evacuation scheme designated Children's Overseas Reception Board (CORB). The convoy left Liverpool on Friday 13 September 1940 and was torpedoed by *U-48* some 600 miles off the west coast of Ireland on 17 September, with the loss of a large percentage of its child passengers. Numbers vary between seventy-seven of ninety children lost, to eighty of 100 children lost. The *Liverpool Daily Post* of 23 September 1940 lists twelve Liverpool children lost. Many of the children evacuated on this convoy were from areas, like Liverpool, most threatened by the enemy and some had already been the victims of the Blitz.

Merchant ships were targeted by both sides and evacuee ships were indistinguishable from those carrying supplies vital to the war effort. After this tragedy, overseas evacuation was largely abandoned, except for those families who made private arrangements.

One of the other ships in that convoy was SS *Duchess of Atholl*. Aboard her was Patricia Burns:

> I went to stay with family friends in the USA – Mr Swint and my father were both employed by ICI and had worked in Buenos Aires together for ten years. Another ship in our convoy, the 'City of Benares', was torpedoed. We sailed into Montreal earlier than expected, having been instructed to go 'Full Steam Ahead'.

This is a controversial point, since it has never been agreed whether or not the *City of Benares* was separated from the convoy. Patricia remembers:

> I returned to England in August 1944. My father, a chemist, had been working in Somerset in a Royal Ordnance Factory making explosives and he and my mother had lived there for four years. Just before returning to Southport in 1945, we spent a holiday in Lyme Regis, and the lady who ran the guest-house had been a passenger with her three children on the City of Benares. Her two daughters were interviewed on TV recently.

This was the Bech family, who featured in a *Timewatch* programme in 2005, sixty-five years after the tragedy. The Bech family survived the sinking of the *City of Benares* and Patricia had been fortunate to be aboard another ship in the convoy.

Like John Johnson, Mavis Luke, née Tidd, who was only three years old in 1939 and lived at No. 1 Bedford Avenue, Melling, describes a narrow escape:

> This is a night (in 1940) that I shall never forget. My father was doing the night shift in the railway signal box. My mother ran out of money for the electric meter and went next-door to a lady named Mrs Yates, who had a daughter, Ettie, who was just going to have a bath. The tin bath was in front of the fire, but she changed her mind when mother and I arrived. The bath was put away and Mrs Yates went to make us all a cup of tea. *This next part is the gospel truth and I live in fear of this story to this very day.* My mother was reading me the story of 'The three little pigs'. As she got to the part where the big bad wolf says 'I will huff and I'll puff and I'll blow the house down' the light went out and there was an almighty bang. As my mother was sitting under a window with me on her knee, she leant forward to protect me. Later, shards of glass

were pulled out of her back. The wardens got us out… we were black with soot and dust. My father came home from work and thought we had been killed. A landmine had dropped on 1, Bedford Avenue. My parents lost everything, but if we had been in there, we would have lost our lives.

This graphic escape depended entirely on Mrs Yates' hospitable nature and Ettie's willingness to forgo her bath, but it is the strange and horribly appropriate moment in the story when the bomb drops that remains in the memory, as it has clearly done for Mavis.

Derek Finney also recalls an amazing escape:

During the Blitz of 1941, my grandmother, Annie Wade, who lived in Empire Street, Litherland, used to walk to her friend's house in Bosworth Street before the siren went each evening and they would then go to the air raid shelter under Bryant and May's Matchworks on Linacre Road. One evening, the siren went early as she was approaching Bosworth Street. When she arrived, she found her friend's front door open but no-one in the house (apparently, when the siren went, her friend had gone next door). My grandmother went into the house and, because her friend's purse was on the table, she stayed there until the 'All-Clear' went. That night, a land-mine fell on the match-works, killing most of the people in the shelter underneath – the one night when my grandmother and her friend had not used it!

Derek remembers another incident in that same year, when he was only nine years old:

The destruction of St Andrew's Church Hall, Litherland (by two heavy high explosive bombs) had a great effect on me. This was the place where I went to Sunday School every Sunday. After this, Sunday School classes were held in the church opposite. The bomb site remained a blank spot on Linacre Road until 1963, when a new Memorial Hall was declared open by the Bishop of Liverpool.

Bryant & May's Matchworks – a fortunate escape for Derek Finney's grandmother!

Derek was later to meet his future wife at the youth club, started in 1947, which assembled in the vestry because there was no church hall.

Harold Russell was less than three years old in 1941 and remembers nothing of the May Blitz, except the family lore that describes the split-second timing that saved his life. He was fortunate in that his mother, Lilian, was not one of those who left a child to cry:

> I was always told that my bed was under the window in the living room, and that I had begun to cry and my mother came and picked me up, and, almost immediately, the window was broken and a chunk of shrapnel lay on the pillow where my head had been only moments before.

This was not the only occasion when Harold remembers enemy planes arriving so swiftly that no warning was given:

> I remember being in the garden with planes going overhead. Suddenly, the chap next door, who was in the RAF, said 'That's not one of ours!' and we all went for cover – I remember seeing a Spitfire chasing the plane away – you could see the flames from its guns.

Rosalind McArt was ten in 1939; she was an only child and lived with her parents, an aunt and her grandmother. Rosalind was in Liverpool throughout the war and remembers a narrow escape during the May Blitz of 1941:

> In 1941, we moved to a house in the next road because it had electricity. One night, we took refuge under the stairs. I passed the time reading, my Dad having rigged up a light. There was a particularly loud explosion, which shook us up somewhat! My Mum gave me a drop of whisky! Next day (or later that same day) we were stunned to find that a bomb had landed outside our former home and only a few yards away. We might all have been killed or badly injured.

Maureen Sheehan, née West, remembers leaving Liverpool in the nick of time, and later being joined by her grandmother:

> My mother, auntie, cousin and myself (aged seven) went to live in Shawforth, near Rochdale, just before the bad Blitz when a land-mine flattened our former home. My sister was in Fazakerley hospital, with diphtheria, and came later. My dad was in the Fire Service in Liverpool and an uncle brought the furniture up in a van with a friend and dumped it inside the door and left it. When we arrived in Shawforth on the train, we had to try to assemble beds, just two children and their mothers, one of whom was pregnant – an Army wife, expecting her second child. Shawforth was near the Pennines, so we found a foot of snow and it was May! My Grandma, a staunch Catholic, thought God would never let anything happen to her and refused to budge, in spite of my dad begging her to join her daughters in safety in Shawforth. That is, until one night when a bomb blast wrapped the window-frame round her shoulders. Gran was on the next train up to Shawforth!
>
> Two more of my Mum's sisters and their families joined us after being bombed out of their homes and they lived in the same back-to-back houses – Heys Buildings in Shawforth. So there were lots of Liverpool kids at St. Anselm's school and we started winning the sports trophies and cups. My cousins, who were old enough, got jobs in the cotton mill. We lived at the top of a hill, or brew, and there was a man who came and knocked my cousins up for work at an early hour with a long stick, which he banged on the bedroom window. When the bombing was over, and we were winning the war, Dad got us a house in Kirkdale and we returned there, having spent a few happy years in safety. Liverpool was devastated. Our new home had

just been patched up and, one night, our bed's bottom legs went through the floor, with my sister and me in it. I think that I can honestly say that we had an eventful time in the war, when asked 'What did you do?'

Lawrence Whittaker, aged four in 1939, was not evacuated because he was very young and also because he had chickenpox when other children were leaving Liverpool:

We lived in Ethiopia Street, near Scotland Road and Stanley Road and, of course, near the docks, so the bombing in our area, where most of my family lived, was fierce. My father was away in the Merchant Navy and my mother, sister, aged three, and I were bombed out twice. The first time, we went to live nearby with our grandparents in their two-up two-down terraced house. It was very crowded and on the night when we were bombed out for the second time, my mother was staying with other relatives further down the street. The blast shook the whole house and my sister and I rushed downstairs and had to climb onto the sideboard to get over the front door, which was off its hinges. We almost slid down the front door – outside there were two unexploded incendiary bombs lying in the gutter. Our Mum was running down the street to us, carried along by the force of the blast, she looked like Superwoman. We were taken into another house, but we were sitting on the couch in a room with no back wall to it. The whole of the back of the house had disappeared. There was a pervasive smell of soot everywhere, which I remember vividly to this day. The whole of one side of the street had gone. Nearby lived our Auntie Jessie – they had a coal-yard with a horse and cart. I remember Auntie Jessie trying to get the frightened horse out of the stable. She was trying to hold its head down and it kept pulling away. It was a big shire horse and she was not a large woman. My Uncle Tom Garner was also bombed. His roof disappeared while he was in bed. I remember standing by and watching the neighbours making a ladder out of some fencing so that they could climb up and get him down. The whole district was on fire. We were lucky that nobody in our family was killed that night because we all lived close together and the bombing that had already taken place meant that we were even more crowded together.

Bill Backshall lacked any real sense of danger:

Clad with the armour of a youthful lack of sense, at the age of fourteen, I stood alone one night in Catherine Street, not far from my home, during a reasonably heavy raid. There didn't appear to be another soul in sight, for most folk had taken the sensible precaution of retiring to the safety of shelters or under their stairs. My mother couldn't keep tabs on me all the time, with her having such a large brood, and she and my sisters were in our home-made shelter. Out of her sight and control, I wandered around the local streets at will, foolishly as I now see, during those deadly night attacks. The only people abroad in the dark night were ARP men, policemen, firemen, German bombers and stupid young boys.

Standing there, my head was cocked toward the river estuary, the direction that the bombers always approached from, and, eventually, I selected one that seemed to be bearing directly on our particular area. Still unconcerned, I paid particular attention as the threatening off-beat drone of the heavily taxed engines grew louder, until the plane was overhead. Spellbound, I stood there, unable to move but somehow sensing what was about to happen. The engine's beat quickened with relief as the aircraft discharged its cargo and at the same time, I identified another sound. It grew louder until it blotted out the bomber's noise altogether. It started as a shrill high whistle, deepening until it became a scream, then it intensified until it became a much louder frightening scream and then, during the last few seconds of its descent, it sounded like lumps of concrete clattering down a corrugated iron roof, a fast, swishing horrible noise.

I followed the noise of the falling bombs just a few yards away, shooting over my head and over the roof-tops facing me, until they struck targets out of sight. It only took seconds for them to fall, but, even so, the noise they made cleft the air apart and registered in my brain for life. There were explosions all around, with the defensive Ack-ack gunfire in full cry, and with the stick of bombs bursting. One bomb buried itself in the pavement thirty of forty yards away but did not explode immediately, which, later, caused one of the more humorous incidents of my war. They weren't as lucky two hundred yards back, where a bomb from the same stick exploded on houses on the corner of Palmerston Drive and a schoolboy chum of mine lost his mother, sister and his home in one moment. Nowadays, I wonder what would have happened if the bomb aimer had pressed his release gear a split second earlier, but then, I just shrugged the whole incident off with the closed imagination of youth.

But this lucky escape was not enough to drive Bill into the shelter. However, he does remember the time when the reality of war began to be thrust upon him:

With an inability to grasp the seriousness of the times, all was very well with my youthful world, until the raids intensified. During one attack, I stood with my eldest brother, Mark, talking to a friend of his at the doorway to his home. This was in Hand Street, a hundred yards from our own rear entrance door. Soon we could hear one particular plane approaching rather low directly towards us. We could sense what was coming for, as the conversation stuck in our throats, we could hear a stick of bombs falling ominously in our direction. Mark and myself started to sprint for home and the friend hurriedly closed the door behind us. Within a few seconds, the bombs were so close we had to throw ourselves against the gable end of the terrace as they struck and exploded one after the other. One struck exactly where we had stood talking, the house and surroundings demolished in billows of dust and, when we scrambled to our feet, Mark chased me straight home. To this day, I never found out how his friend fared. I never asked. I don't think I wanted to know.

Chapter Four

'It might as well have been Australia!'

Some children lived in parts of Merseyside that were considered 'safe' and received evacuees into their homes. It is too simplistic, and, indeed, inaccurate to classify such safe areas as middle-class and to assume that children coming from the 'danger areas' were all deprived or even working-class, although some chroniclers of evacuation have made these assumptions. There were many hard-working, ordinary people in the countryside around Liverpool, and there were people in comfortable circumstances living nearer to the city, especially in the larger houses in Bootle. Nevertheless, there were differences in lifestyle and expectations that were thrown into sharp contrast when living in the same house. There were also prejudices, which are most evident when hearing the stories of children who were evacuated to Southport, and the stories of children who lived in Southport and whose parents received evacuees from Bootle and Liverpool.

Despite the few miles between Bootle and Southport, one area in great danger and the other considered 'safe', the gulf in understanding is very clear in the memories of M. Wilson, six in 1940:

> My parents ran a small private hotel with ten bedrooms, so we ended up with twenty evacuees with their mothers, from three families. The fathers all worked in the Liverpool docks. On one occasion, one of the evacuees had her birthday party and her mother invited me to join them. Uncertain, my mother let me join in and I was amazed at what happened. The family had saved all the coupons for weeks to provide the spread; it looked splendid. The mother, a rather voluptuous lady dressed in black with a shawl over her shoulders, stood at the head of the table and shouted 'Attack!' and every single crumb from the piled-high plates vanished – each child had a full plate – I hadn't had a crumb. Even now, when our family has a get-together, we still say 'Attack!' jokingly. When the families went home, we never heard from any of them, or knew what happened to them – if they survived the war or anything.

It probably did not occur to any of the families to keep in touch with each other. This is also the case for Doreen Dalrymple, although her family's evacuee appeared to be happy for two years. Doreen, eight in 1939, lived in Southport and remembers the arrival of Marlene, who was not contacted by her parents during her stay:

> I vividly remember her coming to our house. An official came to the door and asked my mum did she have a girl or a boy, and we got Marlene for two years… After the war she departed and we've never set eyes on her since. She did settle though and was happy with us.

Unlike Marlene, fourteen-year-old Betty Patten, née Wylie, from Bootle, did not settle in Southport, but took matters into her own hands and brought an end her short but unhappy stay:

> Dinner was a dinner plate of doorstep pieces of bread and one small pot of beef spread between four girls as the main meal of the day. Above the empty fireplace, in November, was a pokerwork plaque 'Initiative – the doing of the right thing without being told.' I didn't need anything else, did I? Got my case, my sixpence – all the money I had – and left. Got the bus and told the conductor to take me as far as my sixpence would allow, which he did. I still had a long walk in the blackout and got home about 11 p.m. 'What are you doing here?' I refused to be evacuated again.

Sometimes, the incompatibility of evacuees and host families caused unhappiness on both sides. Brenda Pearson was seven when the war began and lived in Southport, which was initially seen as a safe area:

> I remember quite vividly a lady coming to our house in Clive Road with three evacuees. My mother had five children at the time and (although I didn't know it) was expecting another one. Where she put the evacuees I don't remember, but she must have found beds for them. I'm afraid the poor things didn't fit in at all and were very unhappy; they didn't speak like us and we didn't know what to make of them; they seemed very rude and had no table manners and I thought they were very scruffy. And then they were no longer there. My mother and father had to go and tell the police they were gone. They were found with other evacuee friends walking along the beach trying to get back to Liverpool.

It is possible to conclude from this memory that the evacuees were equally as unhappy with the situation as Brenda seems to have been. Yet Margaret Barber, Brenda's older sister, aged eleven in 1939, remembers that her family, and especially her mother, did their best for the evacuee guests:

> Our mother took in three little boys, the eldest was only ten years old. We tried to talk to them and be friendly, but they looked really unhappy. I remember we were having plums and custard at teatime and they wouldn't eat it so we asked them what they had to eat at home and they said 'Chips'. We were miles from a chippy, so the next day, my mother made chips for us all.

Margaret remembers their evacuees' attempt to go home, 'The police found a crowd of children trying to get back to Bootle along the beach. I still have a sad feeling for them when I think of it. My mother was very upset for them. They must have been so afraid so far from home and family.'

Some evacuees from Bootle to Southport were happy, although at first it was all very confusing for five-year-old twins, Fred and Helena Smith. Fred remembers:

> In those days children were seen and not heard, so we knew very little of what was going on around us. When we arrived in Southport, we thought it was going to be a wonderful day out. Not realising this day was going to last three years. The first night was one I will always want to forget, but next day we were greeted by an elderly couple, Mr and Mrs Kerr, who we later came to know and love as Aunty Nin and Uncle Jack. In the time we shared their home, they showed us a love and affection we will never forget. They never had children of their own, but what a fantastic Mum and Dad they would have made. During our evacuation, our Mum and Dad came every weekend, only one week they did not come and that was the weekend of the May Blitz.

I have always retained a great love for Southport. I did not know then how near it was: at the time, children were not as wise as they are now – it might as well have been Australia.

Another happy period of evacuation to Southport was experienced by thirteen-year-old Irene Stephenson:

It was in the autumn of 1938 that the situation in Europe became rather worrying. German forces had occupied Czechoslovakia and there was talk of war. After the British Prime Minster, Neville Chamberlain, travelled to Munich to meet the German Chancellor, Adolf Hitler, and came back proclaiming 'Peace in our Time', people reacted in various ways. Some breathed a sigh of relief; others said that the agreement wasn't worth the paper it was written on. Some settled back into their daily routine, but others began to make preparations. The school that I attended was one of these.

Irene was a pupil at Bootle Grammar School for Girls on Breeze Hill and, like the pupils of some other secondary schools, was to find that she benefited from the good organisation and control exercised by the school over the whole undertaking:

My parents received a letter asking whether, in the event of war, they wished their child to be evacuated. After some discussion, they decided 'Yes' and returned the form, duly signed. In early February 1939, all those girls whose parents had agreed were given letters to take home. These said that there would be rehearsals for evacuation and that each girl was to take to school a small case containing some listed items, including a spare school blouse, underwear, socks, night clothes, toothbrush, facecloth and comb. When we arrived at school our cases were checked by the form mistress. We then put on our coats and hats and went out into the playground to form a long crocodile. We all walked from school to Bootle Railway Station in Oriel Road. Having got there, we turned round and walked back again.

During the next few months, this rehearsal took place three more times; cases checked, walk to station, back to school. Then we broke up for the summer holidays. But the political situation became very black indeed. It was announced on the radio that Friday, 1st September was to be Children's Evacuation Day. On the Thursday, we received word to go to school immediately for final instructions. There, we were told to return at 11 a.m. next day, complete with cases, ready to go. And, most importantly, there were to be NO MOTHERS accompanying us! When I arrived home, my mother said 'I'll come to see you off.' 'Oh, no, no, no!' I said. 'No mothers are allowed.' My mother simply said 'Oh, I see', but, privately, she had other ideas.

Friday 1 September dawned – goodbyes were said all round. My father went to work, with, I think, a heavy heart. He had served four years in France during the First World War and was vainly hoping that something would happen to stop another war beginning. Off I went to school, where we all met up together. Our form mistress, Miss Graham ticked names off on her list. We were each given a brown paper carrier-bag which contained a packet of Jacob's Cream Crackers, a tin of corned beef, a packet of tea, a small jar of marmalade and one of jam and a few other things. Carrying our cases and carrier-bags, once again, we formed our crocodile and set off for Bootle Station. A big gate had closed off the station from all but us girls. However, nearby, peering through some railings, was a small group of mothers, including mine. Those of us who saw our mothers were furious, because of the 'No Mothers' rule, and we looked the other way, pretending not to see them, although they were waving to us. So, there were no tears, no clinging goodbyes.

The 'No Mothers' rule was clearly effective in its purpose of preventing emotional and prolonged partings, but it is difficult not to feel sorry for those ignored mothers, no doubt wondering when, or even if, they would see their daughters again! But this incident also illustrates the respect that children had for the authority of schools and teachers, which must have helped to make the huge undertaking of mass evacuation possible. Irene continues:

The train was waiting, we all stepped on, took our seats, and off we went into the unknown. The train stopped at Birkdale Station and, again, we formed our crocodile and walked from the station, over the level crossing, following our form mistress, Miss Graham, to the top of Alma Road, where we were told to stop. I was next to last in the line of 'twos', but when we stopped, Miss Graham told us to right-about-turn, so that those of us who were last, became first. We stood, apprehensively watching Miss Graham begin knocking on the doors of houses on the opposite side of the road. At the first two, there was no reply, but from house number ten came a small middle-aged lady, slim, grey-haired. Miss Graham came over to the line of girls and said 'The first four who want to be together' Our hands shot up and the first two couples, Doris, Elsie, myself and another Irene, walked across the road to be greeted by this lady, Miss Mather, who took us into her home. We had arrived! It was Journey's End!

Irene remembers:

We stayed with her only four months because the school returned to Bootle in May 1940. Many girls had already gone home because they were very unhappy and, of course, there had been none of the expected air raids. They began later when we were back in Bootle! But, during our time in Southport, we had lived in a home-from-home.

Ormskirk, a small market town set in pretty countryside known as 'the salad bowl of England' and fifteen miles from Liverpool, was another place receiving evacuees from the city.

Evelyn Davies, from Derby Street Fire Station, Bootle, arrived in Ormskirk as an evacuee. She was one of those children who could see for themselves that their home was in

Bootle Grammar School girls in Birkdale. From left to right, back row: Irene Stephenson and Doris Tyson. Front row: Irene Parr and Elsie Fairhurst.

danger from enemy action. Evelyn, aged ten in 1939, recalls a charmed world that was suddenly an integral part of the war at home:

> At that time, I lived in the Fire Salvage Station on Derby Street, Bootle with my parents. My father was a fire officer and our home was one of the apartments in the building. There were about half a dozen other firemen and their families living there too. The Liverpool Docks were within walking distance and very vulnerable to attack in wartime.
>
> Looking back, life was quite idyllic, inasmuch as I was part of a circle of childhood friends living in our own little world. We all played together in one of the big yards at the back of the station, not getting in the way of the hard-working men who were very tolerant of us children. Yes, it was a special kind of existence living with the day-to-day running of the Fire Station. The sounds of the fire alarm, the clanging of the engine bell, the hosing down of the appliances, the polishing of all the brasses, and keeping the yards spick and span were all part of the firemen's daily routine. They even arranged Christmas parties for us all with a big tree and presents. That took place in the 'Engine Room' minus the fire engine, which would be moved out, of course.
>
> It was the wireless that gave us news of war breaking out and the atmosphere was sombre in my home. Although I was an only child I don't remember feeling too frightened at the prospect of having to be evacuated, even though I had never been away from home. I was glad that some of my friends would be coming with me to wherever that would be, which turned out to be Ormskirk, and I didn't even know where it was!
>
> The journey, by train from Sandhills Station, did not take long and we alighted at Ormskirk railway station. We were then formed into a 'crocodile' and walked in twos down Derby Street. I remember some of us commenting on the little terraced houses and comparing them to the bigger 'posh' houses. Some of us said we hoped we did not go to this or that house – feeling a bit particular, I suppose! There would be one or two people, mainly housewives, outside each house, probably weighing us all up, and seeming to make an instant decision on which children to take. So one or two of us children would vanish from the 'crocodile' as we trudged along Derby Street, carrying bags or haversacks on our backs, and with our gas masks dangling from a cord over our shoulders. We must have all felt nervous as we had no choice who would take us.
>
> My friend, Audrey Jump, and I walked along with the others and we felt delighted when Mr and Mrs Pope, who had a sweet shop in Derby Street, took the two of us. We had stuck together, as friends do, but Audrey's sister, Pat, had to go to another couple round the corner from us. When Audrey's mother found out, of course, she said 'Why didn't you stay with your sister?' Mr and Mrs Pope, whose son was in the Air Force, also had their daughter-in-law from down south, with her baby, who had come to escape the London Blitz. This led to my first lesson in ironing. I was allowed to iron the baby's clothes and to take it for short walks in its pram. So I felt really grown-up.

In Maghull and Lydiate, during the May Blitz, the two villages absorbed a greater number of evacuees and trekkers than their existing populations. Many people stayed in farm buildings or were taken in by local families. There seems to have been a stronger feeling in these villages that the evacuees and trekkers were escaping from a real danger – older people in Maghull and Lydiate have very clear and painful memories of watching the fires over Liverpool. Interestingly, many of the people who have shared their wartime memories and who now live in Maghull, Lydiate, Burscough and Ormskirk, came as evacuees and returned to settle as adults.

Most trekkers just walked away from danger, but Olive Serridge, thirteen in 1939, remembers travelling in style:

Evelyn (Evie) Davies with her father, fire salvage officer John Courtman, in front of Derby Street Fire Station, Bootle.

Evelyn Davies (with doll and pram) and Dorothy Mitchell, also a fireman's daughter.

My father worked for a bread firm; the firm suggested that the drivers take home the big vans away from the bakery at night. We drove out into the countryside, away from Orrell Park, and slept in the big van some nights.

There was also an official evacuation programme for children. My mother, Ena Brown, was still Ena Sendall in 1939. She died in 1993, but had recorded her memories some time earlier. She was involved in the evacuation of children to Maghull in two ways. As Captain of Maghull St Andrew's Guide Company, she was involved with the actual process of evacuation:

Most of the children came from the south end of Liverpool around the Granby Street area – on the actual day of evacuation, they came into Sefton station (on the Cheshire Lines) and the local Cubs, Brownies, Guides and Scouts had been called in to help and to make them feel at home. We were all on the platform and as the children got off the train, their luggage was taken by a youngster in the Guides or Scouts. In some cases, it was rather funny because you would see quite a small Brownie or Cub struggling along with the case of a much larger child. But it had been impressed upon the local children that they were lucky because they could stay at home, and that the evacuees had to be looked after. The children came up out of the station and across to what used to be a field for Sunday School picnics, where they were gathered together and given something to eat and drink.

Later, some of the people who had agreed to take a child came to collect them in cars. Other children were taken to the houses where they were to stay. Some people were 'choosy', saying 'Have you got a little girl?' or 'I'll take this child' about an apparently quiet and clean-looking child, but others were willing to take any child and, sometimes, more than one child. As time went by, and especially when there was little bombing, some children went home, but those who stayed were integrated quite well into the area – quite a few little girls joined Guides or Brownies, according to their age. Some children stayed forever with their foster-parents. Perhaps something had happened to their own parents – that I don't know! But some did settle here to a very different life to what they had been accustomed to in the city, as Maghull was much more rural then.

Ena Sendall, Maghull's Guide Captain, led her Guides in making evacuees welcome.

My mother was also a member of the Civil Nursing Reserve, based at the First Aid Post in Maghull Institute. Some of the evacuee arrivals had been found to have infectious diseases, such as scabies, and they were treated initially at the First Aid Post. There was also an outbreak of whooping cough during the early part of the war and some of the children were isolated at the First Aid Post and nursed there, until they could either go home to their mothers or they were well enough to return to their foster homes.

Jean Greenhalgh, née Hopegood, was one of the children who arrived in Maghull that day. Although she was only six, her memories echo some of my mother's recollections. Jean recalls:

Sefton railway station, where children from the Granby Street area arrived in Maghull.

I was born at 59, Eversley Street, Liverpool, in 1928. We lived over Hilda's, a Ladies' Dress Shop in Granby Street. I was from a family of eight children and Margaret and I were the youngest. I went to Granby Street School in 1933 and, in 1939, my sister, Margaret, aged six, and I, aged eleven, went to live in Maghull. On the day of the evacuation, there was a lot of noise, getting all the children into orderly lined of 'twos'. There were lots of grown-ups saying goodbye, waving and tears, hugs and kisses, and cries of 'Be good!' We didn't have a lot of clothes to carry and there were bags of all shapes and sizes. My mother gave me a bag of comics that I could hardly carry and I gave a lot away. We were also given Hi-Li bats (a small wooden bat with elastic and ball attached) which we all loved. We walked along Granby Street to Upper Parliament Street to go by tram-car to Exchange Railway Station to board the train for Maghull. We did not know where we were going at all – the journey seemed like ages. When we arrived at the station and got out, Celia Kenny and I looked at each other and said 'This is where we come for Sunday School picnics!', although we had no idea how far we were from Liverpool. Some children thought we were in Scotland – it seemed so far. Celia and Alma Kenny lived in Ponsonby Street and they were my friends. Celia and I still meet. We were taken to the field opposite and went into big tents to be checked… between your fingers, in your hair – we got through all right. I am not sure whether we were given something to eat and drink, but I feel as though we did. Then we were given some food in a brown paper bag to take to the house where we were going. There was various transport – Celia and Alma Kenny and Margaret and I went in a lorry to The Crescent, where we heard people saying 'Two boys or two girls, or even one child'. Celia and I agreed to look for one another, but Celia and Alma went home about two weeks later.

Margaret and I were taken by Mrs Surtees to a lovely bungalow, where we had a drink of milk and a biscuit before settling down for bed. We met Mr Surtees and the dog, Trixie. We had never had a dog, so it was strange, but we loved it eventually. They were the kindest people and looked after us very well. We began to call them Uncle Tom and Auntie Girlie.

A child with gas mask on the Leeds-Liverpool Canal towpath, with the Red Lion bridge in the background. The loaded barges indicate that the canal was an important link for trade and communication.

Ena Sendall, sitting on the bottom step (right), with colleagues from the ARP and Nursing Auxiliary outside Maghull Institute, Damfield Lane.

My sister was always falling in the brook – there had been going to be houses built nearby, but the building had stopped because of the war. Children we made friends with used to jump over the mud, but Margaret was only six, and kept falling in. Poor Mrs Surtees, washing all the mud out of our clothes. My sister went back home to Mum early. Was it the mud? I missed her being there and asked could I go home too. This was a mistake on my behalf; after a temporary stay at home, Margaret joined a family called Yates, in Clent Avenue, because the raids had started. After my stay at home, I went to the same address as my sister. I made a friend with the eldest daughter, but my sister and I were very homesick. After a while, I wrote and asked my mother to take us home, which she did.

During Jean's stay in Maghull, she and the other children in her age group attended Deyes Lane School, where they were photographed along with local children and the class teacher, Miss Lawrence. Jean remembers 'Miss Lawrence took Physical Exercise and I have forgotten what else. I remember her with great fondness as she was always very kind to me.' Amongst the other children in the class was Leonard Rossiter, the actor, who gave us the unforgettable Rigsby and Reggie Perrin. Leonard also lived in Eversley Street and, at home, attended St Margaret's High School, Anfield.

There were some differences in lifestyle and behaviour, but, as pointed out by my own mother, the local children in Maghull and Lydiate had been made very aware that they were fortunate to live in a relatively safe area and need not be separated from their families. There was also, in some instances, a real effort made at understanding the incomers by the adults with whom they stayed.

Ronald (Ron) Rigby was five years old in 1939 and lived in Lydiate. He remembers the village school:

One day, there were more pupils than desks. Mr Dawber, the head-master came in and asked 'How many pennies are there in five shillings?' I was able to answer and was moved up to Standard I to make room for the influx of evacuees from Liverpool. There were about seventy local children and thirty or so evacuees. They were tougher than us, and, though we were generally bigger, they could beat us in playground fights. They ate sugar butties, an unheard-of filling to me. My grandparents, farming at Halsall, took in two little girls, aged about seven or eight. When they looked out of the window, they saw the wash-house and asked 'Who lives there?' These children wanted to walk about while eating their meals – it turned out that at home there were six children and only four chairs. There were people living in an old tram

Deyes Lane School photograph showing evacuees and local children together. Jean Greenhalgh is sitting front row on the right on a chair. Leonard Rossiter is on the left of the back row. The teacher is Miss Lawrence.

Ron Rigby, aged eight, in the garden at Lydiate with his dog, Toby.

at the Rope House, Lydiate, and also in an old furniture van, standing on four barrels, in Bells Lane, Lydiate.

Like Ron Rigby, Harold Gaskell lived in an area that was receiving evacuees because it was rural and, therefore, considered to be safe. However, in wartime, nowhere was completely safe and Harold lived between the Leeds-Liverpool Canal and the Ormskirk-Wigan railway line. Both railways and canals were enemy targets, so there were a number of incidents during Harold's childhood:

> I had two uncles working on the horse-drawn canal boats and my Dad also worked on a large boat in Manchester; he was away all week from Sunday night to Saturday afternoon, so it was a case of us children to help our mother best way we could. My eldest brother was in the army, serving in Burma under General Wingate; they were called Chindits.

The Chindits were a special force trained in commando methods to infiltrate behind Japanese lines in Burma. They were an international force, including British soldiers, Burma Rifles, Hong Kong volunteers, Gurkhas and West African soldiers. The name Chindit was given to them by their leader, Major-General Orde C. Wingate DSO. The Chindit badge included a Chinthe, the symbolic guardian of Burmese temples, half lion, half flying griffin. Harold continues:

> Quite a few children from Liverpool were sent to live in New Lane, and in Burscough, while the war was going on. I soon made pals with some of them. At weekends, I asked some of them to come and play with us, which they did. Later in the year, in September, after dinner-time, I went back to play with them and took with me a bag of apples and gave everybody some; one of the boys asked 'Where did you get those apples?' and I said 'They're

from our garden'. We had apple, pear, plum and damson trees. This boy from Liverpool, and the others agreed, said 'We didn't know apples grew on trees; we only knew they came to the shop in boxes.'

We children used to have little bets on who could see the German bomber planes going over; even though it was night time, we could still see the dark shape of the plane's wing. We could also pick out the German planes from the sound of their engines which was different to ours. One night in 1942, the first wave of German bombers had gone over and the guns had started, with the help of the searchlights picking out the planes, I was walking home on my own from a playmate's house, when I heard a German bomber over New Lane. Next thing I knew was a large 'BANG', a quick flash of light and I was lifted up in the air about four or five feet and then dropped with a heavy bump onto the ground. I got up and ran all the way home and told my mother what had happened. She said a bomb had been dropped near New Lane railway station. Next day, most of the children went to see where the bomb had dropped; there was a hole so big that you could have fitted a whole house in it.

Patricia Blamire was ten years old when the war began and lived in Meols:

I was a pupil at West Kirby High School, as it was then. We were considered to be in a safe area and thus were inundated with evacuees from Liverpool. We accepted a little girl named Joan, possibly about eight years old. All seemed well on her first night until bedtime. But Joan wasn't ready to go to bed until she had had her fish and chips, a regular routine. But that was not in our remit, she would have cocoa with me. No ifs or buts! Mother had made up the spare bed – a divan – but there was a problem. Joan couldn't get under it. Well, she had never slept in a bed, only under one, so that was something new to learn. She also brought the inevitable nits, something I had never encountered before, so my long blonde hair became a thing of the past. Once we had solved these problems, we settled down quite happily for a few months. Mother managed to cut down some of my clothes to fit, a necessity to replace her own. But, after the first wave of bombing, a lot of evacuees were taken home, including Joan. We were sorry to see her go as she had settled in quite well.

Although it was relatively safe when compared with those areas considered most dangerous, the Wirral was very close to Liverpool and the strategic River Mersey with its vital shipping, so there were raids. Patricia remembers:

I used to cycle to school with my friend, Kathleen, and we were always told not to be outside during a raid. One day we were heading home for lunch and the sirens sounded as we cycled along Meols Drive. It was a good excuse to knock on the door of one of the massive houses, where a kindly lady invited us in and gave us lemonade while we waited for the All-Clear to sound.

Patricia also remembers sharing school premises:

At one stage, the pupils from a bombed-out school had to share ours. Somehow, it worked, and we spent some afternoons at one of the large houses nearby for our lessons. There was always a concerted rush for the window-seats as we had never seen them before.

Also living on the Wirral, although not in an area deemed to be safe, was Renee Rose of Pensby Street, Birkenhead. Renee was born in 1929 and she was initially evacuated to Queensferry with her older sister, Joan. Renee remembers:

We got the train from Birkenhead Park, carrying our gas masks and carrier bags with biscuits and things in them. We were taken to a hall where people came to choose us. It was like a cattle market and Joan kept saying that we were together so no-one took us as no-one wanted two children, we were nearly the last to be picked by the Pearsons. I thought they were posh because they had water on the table at mealtimes – at home, we had sarsaparilla!

Although Renee sees the water jug as a marker of social class, some children saw the disappearance of things that they had to eat and drink at home as meanness on the part of their hosts. In fact, such changes were sometimes the result of rationing and the items that disappeared would no longer have been available in their own homes.

Renee's parents, Mabel and Frank Rose, kept her letters and those of her sister, Joan. Renee wrote on the 7 September, only days after being evacuated:

We arrived safe and we had a carrier bag with food for us and we gave it to Mrs Pearson. We got a Nestles milk 4d bar of chocolate and Ideal milk in tins and last, but not least, two bags of biscuits and a tin of corned beef. Mrs Pearson gave us stew for tea on Friday. Could you send me a dress or two and a brooch most of all please. We went black-berrying when we got here. We have got a big garden here – you want to come and see it. Try to come and see us please…

Joan and Renee had an older sister, Vera, who wrote regularly to them with serial stories about Tarzan and Deanna Durbin, then a popular film star. One letter from Joan and Renee ends, 'Please come and see us some time – tell Vera it is only 14 miles from Birkenhead to Queensferry and 28 miles there and back.'

Although Renee tried valiantly not to be too demanding, all her letters show that she misses her parents. However, it cannot always have been easy for parents, sisters and brothers to visit evacuees, as one of the letters makes it clear that hospitality from the foster family was not always forthcoming. Renee's older sister, Joan wrote:

It is alright for you to come on Sunday, but if you come, please bring some tea because Mrs Pearson might have somebody coming to see her and I do not think she wants you to have tea in the house and if you come before dinner, bring dinner, unless you take us to the café across the road.

Queensferry began to experience raids and was not much safer than Birkenhead. Renee wrote home, 'It is dangerous here – we are between two aerodromes and steel works and electrician works and people are taking their children back… COME TO SEE US SOON.' So both girls left Queensferry. Joan soon had her fourteenth birthday, left school and went to work, while Renee went to stay with her Aunt Alice in Chester. Later, the family home in Birkenhead was bombed and Renee's family went to live in Grange Mount, which had been requisitioned and made available for bomb victims.

Eric Wells, seven in 1939, experienced a short period of evacuation to Staffordshire at the beginning of the war, before he went to live with his grandparents at Huyton Quarry when his mother became ill:

In October 1939, we went for a week's holiday to Blackpool, and, whilst there, my parents met a teacher who was on holiday from Brownhills in Staffordshire. She persuaded my parents to let me be evacuated to her parents, in case there was bombing in Liverpool. Miss Thompson's parents lived in Pelsall Lane, Brownhills and her father was head-teacher of the local primary school. In early 1940, Mrs Thompson was taken ill and I went to live with the Deputy Head, Mr Oakes and his wife and young son, Jim, aged about three or four years years old. It was a happy time for me; they had a large garden at the rear of the house, which meant plenty of space for playing.

But by mid-1940, I returned home to my parents, as no bombing had occurred in Liverpool and I returned to Dovedale School. Later, my mother became ill with pleurisy and pneumonia and she was taken to my grandfather's cottage in Tarbock , while I went to my other grandparents in Huyton Quarry. I was in Chapel on the Sunday evening with my grandparents when a friend appeared at the chapel porch – he had come to let my grandparents know that my mother had passed away. I continued to live with my grandparents at Huyton Quarry and travelled every day by Crosville bus to Picton Clock, Wavertree, then by tram to Penny Lane and thence a walk to Dovedale Road School. My time at Huyton Quarry was very happy; plenty of space to play out in the fields, down the lane, opposite my grandparents' house. I remember poor people being brought out in the evening from Liverpool, I think, the Scotland Road area, to avoid the bombing. They slept in St Gabriel's Parish Hall overnight, returning to Liverpool in the morning.

Elva Barooah was only three in 1939, young enough to be evacuated with her mother:

My sister was six years older than me and was evacuated to Skelmersdale, which was quite countrified at the time. I was evacuated to Hoscar, but, as my mother was with me, I don't remember being at all concerned about it. I remember being taken out by some older girls and being totally astonished at seeing great expanses of open fields. My home was in Aintree, working class, very respectable streets of terraced houses, and, of course, I had no experience of any holidays in the country. We stayed in a house that is still there, by a railway level-crossing, which the house-owners – I think, the woman – operated manually. We came home fairly quickly as there wasn't much bombing at first and my mother didn't like leaving my father alone.

Tarvin, near Chester, was the destination for Jean Campbell, née Stevens, who lived in Webster Road, Liverpool, 7 (an endangered inner-city area). Jean was nearly ten when the war began:

I was evacuated from Lawrence Road School with my older sister. I remember my mother couldn't get me a haversack, so I had a kitbag. I remember sitting on a train taking us to our new home – it was exciting! Now I think how the poor parents must have felt – losing their children. We arrived at a hall and the local people picked us out. A lovely lady picked four of us. At the time, we thought Mrs Grimes - that was her name - was old. But, I suppose, being children, anyone over forty to fifty seemed old. Mrs Grimes was lovely – she lived in a cottage and had a son with a mobile grocery round. He stored his goods in a shed in Mrs Grimes' garden. We were allowed to take a chocolate bar sometimes. I always took a Mars bar.

My mother and brother, aged two and a half, were evacuated to Waverton, near Chester, to a beautiful mansion owned by a gentleman farmer, Farmer Lee. He had a housekeeper and a maid. The house was big. It had a nursery, a cider room, stables - and there were three dogs, pigs, cows and horses. My mother managed to get my sister and I with her. We were spoilt rotten, as the house-keeper, a Miss Partington (I think that was her name) was the most beautiful cook. We had the most gorgeous meals – I can still taste them today!

Chapter Five

School Life Away – just like Enid Blyton!

It appears from the stories and memories that children whose whole school was evacuated together along with the staff, and who were kept together for their schooling, had a far better experience than those who were billeted in a more haphazard way across a wider area. These children were sent to the local school with teachers who were strangers to them and in whom they did not feel that they could confide any concerns or unhappiness that they were experiencing. Some children rarely saw their old schoolmates from home if they had been sent to different suburbs of a country town or to different villages. There were many more, quite small schools at that time, so the possibility of children from one Liverpool school, or even classmates, being sent to a number of different country schools was quite high.

This combination of circumstances meant that the pupils of grammar schools, which, in the main, were evacuated as a body to share the premises of a specific school, had the best experience. The Queen Mary High School for Girls was originally in Anfield Road and later had a new building in Long Lane, Aintree. The school was evacuated to Shrewsbury, but was recalled after a relatively short period, initially to share the premises of Holly Lodge High School on Queens Drive, and later to move into their own unfinished building. Both Holly Lodge and the new QM school buildings were in the suburbs, but many girls lived nearer to the most dangerous areas. It is fortunate that one of the ways in which QM celebrated its Golden Jubilee in 1960 was to produce a special edition of the *School Magazine*. Contributions, in the form of their memories of school days, were invited from former members of staff and 'old girls'. These have provided a rich source of material recalling the experience of a whole-school evacuation from every point of view, including the Headmistress at the time. The difficulties and the humorous moments of moving into an unfinished building in war-time are also recalled in various accounts. Miss D. Grayson took up her new appointment in September 1939, taking over from Miss Adams, who had a new post elsewhere, but was present on evacuation day. Miss Grayson was head of QM until 1944, when she was succeeded by Dr Liddle. So Miss Grayson saw almost the whole of that momentous period with one school. It is worth reading the memoir that she produced in 1960.

Miss Grayson wrote:

First day of the Autumn term 1939, but how strange the circumstances, for it was early on Sunday morning and instead of assembling in the school hall, staff, girls and a new headmistress were waiting in the courtyard of the old QM building for the trams which were to carry us to the station, to the train, to Shrewsbury – to evacuation. I can still see the scene; the sea of unknown faces (among them one of the new children clasping her doll, her sheet anchor in all the strangeness) and the anxious crowd of parents waiting to see us go, torn between the misery of parting from their daughters and their relief at the knowledge that, at least, they would be safe from danger. I remember feeling deeply touched by the cheer which they raised as Miss Adams and I led off. It expressed, I think, their gratitude and their confidence in the staff to whom they were committing the charge of their children. I was filled with a sense of deep responsibility, for I knew that it would not be easy for me a stranger, to help children that I did not know to face such an unprecedented experience.

We were fortunate – and unfortunate. Unfortunate in that Shrewsbury was too accessible to Liverpool, and in the months of freedom from danger ahead families found the strain of living apart unbearable, so that after each weekend visit from parents there were always some girls who went home; or staff returning from weekends off duty, would meet cyclists pedalling sternly towards Merseyside. For girls who had not come with us and for those who had gone home, classes were organised by Miss McMechan in the old school building (Anfield Road) and girls did make eager use of that opportunity.

Miss Grayson became Headmistress of Queen Mary High School for Girls in 1939.

But for those who managed the adjustment to life in evacuation, Shrewsbury was a fortunate second home. Life in a small proud county town steeped in tradition, deeply rooted in the surrounding countryside, revealed to city girls an older England and taught them, I think, to appreciate a slower, perhaps steadier, rhythm of living – and when home seemed far away, there was the reassuring familiarity of Woolworth's to comfort one. Unkind rumour declared that if one wanted to make sure of finding a girl on Saturdays one had only to visit that busy social centre!

We were fortunate too in our hostess school. How generously they concealed their dismay at having to share their new building with us, before they had had time to use it themselves, and if the air which blew straight from those Welsh hills on to the open corridors curdled the blood in our veins, what a compensation that breathtaking view was. We had one of the loveliest Autumns that I can remember and senior girls were quickly recruited for potato picking under Miss Dodd's leadership and came back sunburnt and healthy, even if groaning with stiffness. Juniors had some lovely Saturday expeditions with Miss Hothersall. I wonder if they remember how we gasped with delight as we caught sight of a herd of spotted deer browsing in a park land.

The winter was one of the hardest I remember but snow in Shrewsbury was very different from the snow we knew in big towns, and remained white and crisp for weeks. PT classes went sledging with Miss Barrow and Miss Stevenson and came back rosy and sparkling with vitality.

I remember that in the first days at Shrewsbury I was deeply impressed by the mature and responsible attitude of 'Queen Mary's' Sixth Formers. Their sturdy acceptance of the difficulties was a great example to the school.

To the present girls of 'Queen Mary' those wartime days must seem part of a distant bad fairy tale but the spirit in which staff and girls faced the difficulties brought, I think, a happiness just as deep as that which comes to the more privileged girls of post-war school life. The pages which they wrote into the story of the School will prove I hope in this Jubilee Year to have been not unworthy of the rest.

It is clear that the energetic young staff worked hard in Shrewsbury and at the new school in Long Lane to create as normal a school life as possible and to make the war years not just bearable but fun for the girls in their charge. But it is also sobering to realise that this is the generation of women whose chances of marriage and children of their own had been damaged by an earlier war. Some of their memories are also interesting as they offer a more informal view. Miss Abbatt and Miss Barrow recalled the coldness of the open-air corridors at Shrewsbury, where Miss Norman attended prayers in fur gloves and the form room doors froze up so that a few days holiday were necessary.

Muriel Love, née Hodson, (QM 1937-1944) paints a vivid and detailed picture of evacuation to Shrewsbury, which she clearly treated as an exciting, schoolgirl adventure:

When in 1939, we were evacuated, the remarkable thing was the complete lack of panic, surely a tribute to parents and staff. With rucksacks, and white pompoms pinned to our hats for easy identification, we set off on our mystery journey, which brought us to Shrewsbury. There, at an improvised clearing station, we were each issued with a carrier bag containing emergency ration, including corned beef and a large block of chocolate. With these additional burdens, we set off in groups to areas of the town assigned to us, and trailed from house to house, losing one or two members at each, until all were accommodated... Not all placings were immediately successful, but after some reshuffling, a fair degree of stability was achieved.

This is one of the ways in which children involved in whole-school evacuation were fortunate. These 'reshufflings' would have included consultation with the staff who knew their own pupils. Unlike those children who were accompanied only by one or two teachers from home, if any, children involved in whole-school evacuation gained some security from the presence of familiar adults. More than one child involved in a whole-school evacuation has remarked that, despite staying in private homes, the communal activities, which continued at weekends, made their evacuation experience 'just like Enid Blyton'.

Muriel continues:

I was extremely fortunate in being placed with another member of my class in an excellent home where we were treated with kindness and understanding, and very well fed. Our foster family had a tortoise and five cats – no strays were ever turned away. Perhaps that is why two evacuees were accepted so philosophically.

Saturdays were great fun. Without a care, we would walk round the town eating plums from the bags, peanuts by the half-pound and tablets of jelly from the paper. This... extended to large overdoses of cod-liver oil and malt, consumed secretly in our bedroom after meals.

I now appreciate how much the staff did to keep us happy and occupied. The outstanding excursion for me was the pilgrimage to Uriconium, organised and led by Miss Hothersall, on bicycles one glorious Saturday afternoon. The deep snow and frozen river thrilled us in winter. Liverpool could offer nothing like this. It was on the icy

Miss Norman, QM's Maths mistress, accompanied the school to evacuation in Shrewsbury.

road that I fell off my bicycle, broke a leg, and so had to go home to my parents. Before I could walk again the school had returned to Liverpool. We little realised that the danger from air raids was by no means over.

Like the Queen Mary High School, Waterloo Park School was an all-girls establishment. Muriel Wrench, who had been one of its pupils, moved to Prestatyn with her family after the May Blitz of 1941:

The most difficult part of moving to Prestatyn was transferring to Rhyl High School. Changing from an all girls to a mixed one was hard – the subjects were streamed differently and I found myself in a Science class – three girls and the rest boys. Masters who shouted and threw blackboard wipers across the room. We giggled at the number of times two boys seemed to spend their days outside in the corridor.

Country schools were very different in style and size from the schools that most Liverpool children had attended. Some children were able to experience a different way of life at first hand because of the arrangements their parents made for them. Betty Harrison (née Capstick), twelve years old when the war began, went, along with her brother, aged ten, and sister, aged six, to stay with her aunt and uncle in Howgill, near Sedbergh, Kendal:

Just a few days after war was declared, we travelled by bus from Lime Street bus station and a taxi from Kendal. My relations had a farm, we helped with the harvest, picking potatoes and bringing bracken off the fells by sledge with horses. We all went to Howgill school – just about ten pupils and one teacher. We had a long walk each day with a packed lunch, wet or fine, no other transport. I remember when we were in Howgill School, the dentist coming and just taking out any teeth, all in the cloakroom, whether we liked it or not.

The journey to school in the countryside was very different from going round the corner through city streets and the winter of 1939 was a hard one. Francis Nelson remembers going to school from the holiday boarding house called 'Fodwen', in Penmaenmawr, where he and his elder brother had been billeted:

We only went to school half a day. We shared with locals morning or afternoon. The school was a long way from 'Fodwen' out on the Dwygyfylchi road. We went on the local red bus. The winter was bad, very cold and we had heavy snow. We got to school; the snow came down in blizzard form and we had to walk back to 'Fodwen'. It was a difficult journey for all the children and teachers. My brother and I were not well equipped clothing-wise and we got good winter clothes from the WVS. We never had parental visits; my dad was in the RAF and I don't think my mum could afford the costs.

Some children had not travelled many miles to evacuation, but they still found life very different. For Evelyn Davies, there were great contrasts between living in Derby Street, Bootle and Derby Street, Ormskirk:

I, along with the other evacuees, attended school in Ormskirk and, for one of our lessons each week, the class was taken into the surrounding countryside. Walking through green fields and then into the woods to pick wild flowers was memorable to a 'townie'. That is where I first learned the names of trees and what their leaves looked like. It was fun for us to collect pine cones, and various leaves to stick in our exercise books. It was a new discovery for myself, and

From left to right: Evelyn Davies with Pat Jump and Pamela Fletcher in the Fire Station yard. The families lived in flats on the landings round the yard, which can be seen at the top left of the picture.

a lot of children, to learn what botany was all about. A local farmer had an orchard full of pear trees and the boys would raid it, and bring back ripe pears for the girls. We thought they were brave when they told us how the farmer had chased them and how they had run so fast he could not catch them!

Benjamin (Ben) Webb was thirteen in 1939 and lived in Tetlow Street, Walton, and was evacuated to stay in the gamekeeper's cottage, 'Crow's Mill', near Alveley village, Shropshire with the Garbett family:

I had never seen so much fruit on trees... Uel (Samuel) was a general handyman and they bred pheasants for the shoot; we had a pig, a dog, hens. School was three miles away and I could run it in no time and sing at the same time – my favourite was 'Strawberry Fair'. I used to run all the messages, over to the farm for the milk; or to the pub by the River Severn to fetch 'ciggys'. My Mum missed me and wanted me home and we hadn't been bombed so, after about six months, I came home. In my last year, I went to five different schools, St Lawrence's, Alveley; Walton Lane; Gwladys Street; Lambeth Road and Priory Road. At seventeen (in 1943) I volunteered for the Navy. I was in Arctic and Atlantic convoys and finished up in the Pacific Ocean alongside the American Fleet.

Ben kept in touch with his host, Uel and his family, and went to Uel's ninetieth birthday party in 1999.

Chapter Six

School Life At Home

The experience of schooling varied greatly during the war years. Initially, schools closed in Liverpool in the expectation that children were to be evacuated. However, when it became clear that many children had stayed at home and that others were returning in increasing numbers, some schools did re-open. But, as the war progressed, schools were damaged or destroyed. There were not enough teachers. Evelyn Davies remembers:

> The Headmaster of my school, along with some of the teachers, had been called up to fight for our country. It was because of the shortage of teachers that schooling became spasmodic and 'home teaching' was introduced. We went to various pupils' houses that were made available through the kindness of their parents. For about a couple of hours each week, we were instructed by a teacher and given homework.

How much home teaching was received is impossible to ascertain. Some groups of parents co-operated to offer some sort of basic education, but other children gained an enormous degree of freedom and spare time and, correspondingly, missed much of the education that they would have received in peacetime. How much was done by parents to bridge the gap left by the lack of formal schooling depended on the circumstances of the family and their attitude to education.

Some parents attempted to help not only their own children, but others too. Olive Woods was seven when the war began. She remembers that she and her young sister, Muriel, only four years old, were not evacuated because her mother 'used to say, if one goes, we will all go.' Her mother decided to make some provision for other children who had stayed at home. 'My Mum took in ten children and opened her sitting-room as a school; our education was limited, but I think we had a better knowledge of things than children today.'

Bedford Road School, Bootle – the classroom clock stopped at the time of the raid.

When Jean Campbell returned to Liverpool from evacuation at Tarvin, near Chester, she found there was a slight increase in the hours of schooling she received, but the time was, like many children's education, limited:

> At Tarvin, we had to go to school across the fields. I think we only had half a day school. When the bombing died down, my parents brought us home and I remember having about two hours a day schooling in a private house with another two or three children. I always think I missed out on the vital years of my schooling.

David Buckley attended St Silas School in High Park Street:

> We were all given letters from the teacher to take home to our parents saying that all the children were being given the chance to be evacuated somewhere out of Liverpool. When I gave it to my mother, she said that my sister and myself would stay at home, and that if we were going to be blown up, we would all go together. I saw all the other children leaving, whose parents had agreed to let them go, with their names on labels pinned to their coats and carrying their gas masks and bags. After they had gone, the school closed and, for a while, there was nowhere to attend, until after about two months, we were told to attend at a house in Rhiwlas Street, where about six of us were taught by a teacher in the front room of the house. When schools began to re-open, I was given the chance to go to either Dingle Vale School or St Margaret's School in Princes Road, which I opted for, until I left at the end of the war, aged fourteen. The school entrance was in Hampton Street; right opposite was where they used to make the barrage balloons. These used a lot of rubber solution, so, when we got out of school, we used to go across and ask the women who worked there if they had any solution that had gone hard. They used to give us a big lump and we were able to have a game of football with it.

Bill Backshall, having been born in 1926, was already in his final year at Lander Road School when war was declared. This is how he remembers what happened when school-children were offered mass evacuation:

> For a few boys of my age group, thirteenish and not too far from leaving school, our grand education was more or less considered complete, so we were not evacuated but left to our own devices. Later, we were remembered by someone in authority who recalled us to the empty school, but it was really only a gesture and a waste of time, for the two young teachers in charge seemed to have other things on their minds and I shouldn't wonder, for they were of military age and France and the Low Countries were being over-run by the enemy. Most days, this small unruly group of young lads were deposited across the playground in a small building that housed a laundry and cookery room, intended for girls' education in normal times. We were left there, unsupervised for hours on end and the result was complete anarchy with wet laundry and partly cooked pastry being flung everywhere.

Marjorie Greenwood had a varied experience of school life during the war. Initially a pupil at St George's School, Everton, she had a short spell at school in Whitchurch: 'Wherever you were sent to, you went to the nearest school, which was full before we invaded them.'

Returning to Liverpool allowed her, at first, to go back to her own school. But then, an unexploded bomb in Havelock Street caused her family to live with her grandmother in Cranmer Street:

While at my grandmother's house, I went to a school called St. James the Less in Hankin Street. It was overcrowded, so sometimes some of us had to go to somebody's house to be taught instead. I even had a different surname while staying at Grandmother's – I was known by my mother's maiden name of Yoxon.

When this house also became unsafe to live in as a result of enemy action, Marjorie's family went to stay with her aunt in Lauriston Road, 'I went to yet another school, this time called Florence Melly, in Grandison Road, off Queen's Drive. Every school I went to taught me differently!'

Ronald Molyneux had been evacuated to Ludlow, but he and his older brother ran away twice, and were then allowed to stay at home:

So we happened to be in Liverpool right through the May Blitz. We classed it as an exciting time. The bombs dropped at night, we searched for shrapnel during the day; as kids swapped marbles years later, we swapped bits of bombs and shells. We still went to school, crunching through glass from shop windows blown out, looking for the odd sweet! Our school, Gwladys Street, didn't fare very well and we got sent home, to our delight, and collecting more shrapnel on the way home. We even found coins welded together with the heat, really good for swaps.

When Austin Gahan returned to Norris Green from Colomendy, his parents were both doing warwork. Luckily, Austin enjoyed school life:

My Dad opted to repair Army lorries as he was a Commercial Vehicle Body Builder. As he was gassed when serving in the 1914-1918 war, he was too old to join in the 1939 war. My Mum worked in the Royal Ordnance Factory (ROF) in munitions at Stopgate Lane and Kirkby and was a tester of the Sten gun. She actually worked in a building next to one that was blown up. She worked two shifts, 6-2 one week and 2-10 the next. My Mum did not come home until 11pm, so I did not see her then. On the 6-2 shift, she was not there when I got up for school. My Dad had also gone to work. He left at 6.30am and had to go by bike to the Docks area. Poor Mum and Dad had to work such long hours! I enjoyed school and I used to stay behind at the Play Centre and I feel this made me more interested in Sport, as we did gymnastics there. And we played football and cricket at Walton Park. We used to get a cup of cocoa at the Play Centre. Later the glass windows were blown out, so we all had to go to different houses for our lessons. As my parents were at work in the evenings – on my way home from school I had to go to a Mrs. Reece, as my Mum had an arrangement with her to look after me. Mrs Reece also had three grown-up daughters who looked after me. When the girls were getting ready to go to The Black Bull, (a local public house), they would put gravy browning on their legs because they could not get any stockings. Then they would get a black line drawn down the back of their legs to look like a seam.

After their initial evacuation to Penmaenmawr, Francis (Nick) Nelson and his brother, Gerry, were back home in Liverpool later in the war:

In September 1942, me and my brother started school properly at the Christian Brothers grammar school, St Edward's College. We passed the entrance examination and my mother paid for us to go to St Edward's. She had won the Easy Six on Littlewood's Pools and paid for us for 1942/3 year. 1943/4, cash was hard to come by; but the 1944 Education Act saved us and we stayed at St Edward's.

Francis and Gerry Nelson must have been intelligent little boys, since they had been evacuated to various different areas and attended a number of different schools. At times, they had

Nick Nelson, (second from right, back row) and the Junior Bants rugby team, St Edward's High School, 1943/44.

only half-days in school, and yet, they were able to pass this examination, and, above all, they were fortunate to have a mother who saw their education as a worthwhile investment.

Travelling to and from school in wartime Liverpool offered many opportunities to see the activities of adults at war. Francis remembers:

> St Edward's is in Sandfield Park, West Derby and during the war our neighbours were the Army Service Corps. The trees in the park were good cover and the army trucks were parked in North and South Drives. Queens Drive (the main ring road round Liverpool) was a main road for wartime traffic and airplane fuselages were carried on RAF vehicles up to Speke from and to the Docks. A good excuse for arriving late at school!

Another boy who passed the examination to enter St Edward's College was Bernard Browne:

> I was eleven years old in 1939, and was due to start at a beautiful new grammar school in Sandfield Park, West Derby. My starting date was postponed; some of the pupils already attending had been evacuated to a safe haven in Wales but all the new entrants like myself remained at home. Was it to have a long extended holiday? Not a bit of it, the Liverpool Education Committee had organised temporary contingency plans whereby some parents had volunteered to allow a limited number of pupils the use of their homes in the day with a teacher giving lessons in these novel and unusual circumstances. Eventually I joined my new school, which was fully functional by Christmas 1939. I was sixteen in 1944 and joined the world of commerce. Adolf Hitler certainly blighted my secondary education years; there were no sports days; no prize giving for academic excellence and no extra-curricular activities.

D. Hartley-Backhouse was ten years old in 1939 and lived in Norris Green. He remembers:

> The day before war was declared, my Welsh grandparents took me to live in the middle of Anglesey, North Wales. For two months, I attended the Welsh village school. Then my grandfather died and my grandmother went to live in Llanfyllin, mid-Wales. I came home and passed the scholarship to attend the Liverpool Institute High School. Despite the bombing, I was never late for school, travelling by tram-car. They all had conductresses, who were busy collecting the fares. If you stood on the platform to ring the bell, you did not have to pay the fare.

Frances Jennings returned home in December 1939 from a short period of evacuation to Chirbury in Montgomeryshire. At first, schools were closed and houses were used as temporary classrooms, but Frances was in the Scholarship class and went in for the review prior to sitting the Scholarship Examination in Liverpool:

The results came out at Easter 1940 and I was to attend Notre Dame Girls' School from 4 August. Uniform was necessary and a list of items required was given. We went to Lewis's in Liverpool to get the winter uniform. When clothes coupons were issued during the next year, extra coupons were given to children of a certain age to allow for 'growing up'.

Notre Dame also had an Infant and Junior School, attended by Joan Stables, aged six in 1939. Joan lived right in the heart of Liverpool, where her father was the tenant of the London Tavern, in Greek Street at the top of Copperas Hill, to the rear of the Adelphi Hotel. This public house is also near Lime Street Station, still a main railway station today. Despite the vulnerable situation of the tavern, Joan, who knew that the adults were discussing evacuation for her, 'pleaded and pleaded with (her) mother not to send her'. Joan's parents agreed that she could stay at home. So Joan was in Liverpool throughout the war years and, in particular, her memories of the May Blitz of 1941 are both sad and frightening. Joan's father had a section of the beer cellar as an air-raid shelter, which to Joan was damp and unpleasant, 'full of beer barrels and a horrible musty smell of beer'. Customers and, if the raid was early in the day, passers-by, would shelter together in these cellars. When the all-clear sounded, Joan's thirteen-year-old brother would go up and make Oxo or Bovril drinks for everyone. Some passers-by might have been hoping for something stronger!

During this period, each morning it seemed to Joan, some children were missing from school and many mornings began with a Requiem Mass for children who had been killed during the previous night's raid. Joan had a little friend, called Joanne, whom she called for each morning to walk to school together. One morning, she found her friend's home reduced to a heap of rubble, cordoned off by wardens. When she arrived at school, Mother Superior told her that Joanne and her mother had been killed in the previous night's bombing. After that, Joan took a longer route to school – Joan said, 'I just couldn't bear to look at the place where my friend had died... I mean, you couldn't, could you?' Joan was eight years old. Despite this sadness, Joan remembers the contrast between the peaceful, polished, ordered interior of the Convent with the filth, confusion and devastation outside. She believes that the calm and unchanging atmosphere and the security provided by the nuns of Notre Dame was beneficial for the pupils.

Winifred Abram, née Abbott, was also educated by nuns, in the Convent Orphanage of the Sisters of Charity, in Leyfield Road, where Mass was attended every morning. Winifred's father had served in the Army in both the Boer War and the First World War. She was sixteen in 1939 and remembers that older girls used to undertake everyday tasks, like setting and clearing tables, but they were also accustomed to sharing the responsibility for the younger children, sometimes taking sick children to Alder Hey Hospital. So, when the Blitz began, it was natural that older girls would help in taking the younger ones to the air-raid shelters. Winifred left school during the war and went to work, cooking for the troops at the Promenade Hospital, Southport, which was used as a military hospital at that time.

Many people who were children at this time had a much more piecemeal experience of education. Joyce Jones, née Roberts, was twelve when the war began. She had started at Sherwoods Lane School in August 1939, and she remembers:

For a short time, school went on as usual. Gas masks were given to everyone, to be carried at all times. We had to practise each day at putting them on and off. Then they decided that school should be closed while air raid shelters were built at the school.

Phil Taylor's memories are of an exciting period of freedom, but this also implies a loss of schooling:

Winifred Abram (second from left) with colleagues at the Promenade Hospital, Southport, a military hospital during the war.

One night while we were in the air raid shelter, the air raid warden put his head in the door and said that St Alphonsus' school was on fire. We all went to that school and when we heard it, we ran out of the shelter and started dancing in the road. We did get a good hiding from the Police and any other adults nearby for leaving the shelter. We could have been killed because bombs were falling all around. I think that was the best thing that happened for us. After that, we only went to school for half-days in some large houses nearby. One week, we would go mornings, and afternoons the next, but we rarely went because nobody could find us. Eventually, the school teachers came to our Mums to find out why we were not at school and then we got a good hiding and were taken to school for a week or two until we went AWOL again. Eventually, the bombing ceased and they found a school not far away that had not been damaged and, much to our dismay, we had to share it with the existing pupils.

Miss Grayson, Headmistress of the Queen Mary High School, recalled the return to Liverpool from the official whole-school evacuation to Shrewsbury:

We were just planning how we should explore the delights of what was obviously going to be an early spring in the Shropshire lanes – when we were recalled to Liverpool. But where were we to go, for our old school must not be used and our new building was not yet ready. Powers of adjustment were certainly kept at full stretch that year, for our hostesses as well as ourselves. No sooner had Holly Lodge begun planning how they would pick up the threads of school life in their own building again than they learnt that they would be invaded by us. They accepted the shift system with great good will, giving us the complete freedom of their building so that 'Queen Mary' too could pick up the threads and feel itself a complete school again, and girls who had remained for me names on the registers of the Liverpool group became real persons. My chief memories of Holly Lodge centre upon their garden which seemed so much part of their school life. The smell of lilies of the valley still calls up for me that wonderful bed in the sunny corner on the way to their Junior House which was to form, in that very odd experience of 'school in August' that was ordained for us, our private headquarters for the activities that replaced lessons.

    The scene that I must confess I cannot remember at all is that of our first Assembly in the new building in Long Lane. I think my memories are over shadowed by all the problems that we faced, for the building was not finished and night bombing had begun. I think we may even not have been allowed to have a large Assembly, for Air Raid warnings became part of the everyday pattern of life and soon we were telescoping our school day into the hours between 10 and 3.30 to allow for extra sleep after the nights spent in shelters and cellars. The hours spent in the school shelters were beguiled with Games and improved with Mental Arithmetic; but tedious though they were, the staff and I could not but be thankful that there was no serious bombing in the daytime. 'Queen Mary' girls were wonderfully steady and calm (I remember how impressed the workmen were at the silence and control with which forms led out when the sirens went) and school work was tackled courageously in spite of fatigue and the distraction of the hammering that went on for at least six months more. By the summer of 1941 raids had come to an end, the building was at last completed as far as it ever would be in wartime, and school life could resume some of its normal character.

I am amazed when I consider how much was achieved in the midst of war-time schooling with its shortages and restrictions. We managed to maintain contact with the School Ship and even had a visit from Captain Watson. Cot collections were as generous as ever in spite of the claims of War Savings and the many new appeals that war-time disasters brought. [The 'Cot Fund' endowed cots at the Ellen Gonner Home for Sick Children in West Kirby] Some of you will remember a happy Saturday afternoon spent at the Ellen Gonner Home (almost my only opportunity to discover and enjoy the sandy beaches I had heard so much of). Dr Wallace and Miss McGibbon kept the Gilbert and Sullivan tradition alive in a joint production with Holly Lodge and Blackburne House

This joint production of 'The Gondoliers' was put on in aid of the Lord Mayor's Red Cross Fund. Miss Grayson continued:

Miss Rabson saw to it that the war-time generation of QM girls did not miss the opportunity to learn how to act and interpret character. Androcles and the Lion in particular proved an excellent choice for schoolgirls with its mixture of seriousness and fun. Some of my most vivid memories are of the Christmas Parties for the Special Schools' children and the panto-mimes which the Upper V traditionally produced for them. A chorus of charwomen led by Zena Cristal would have done credit to the professional stage with their topical allusions to various wartime campaigns and their catchy tunes. I am glad too not to have missed QM's famous musical skipping, a feature of the Gym Displays which we kept going.

Holidays for Juniors were a wartime invention which was heartily approved of. It was Miss Abbatt and Miss Barrow who first had the idea and the holiday that they organised with Miss Brennell, Miss Norman and others at Dolgelly (Dolgellau) was such a success that it had to become an annual event, complete with 'midnight feasts' and the traditional escapades of school stories. Senior girls picked peas and in term-time helped with the potato harvest and were introduced at Easter to Youth Hostelling with Miss Dodd. As I survey the varied picture, I feel that the girls of those years missed little of what normal school life gives and gained in addition the enriching experience of service unselfishly given.

Miss Abbatt remembered that when they came home to Liverpool:

Even before term began the new school was hit by a bomb. How we were interrupted by air raid sirens! That first day we couldn't get an assembly – and a day or two later we couldn't begin school dinner because we kept trailing out to the shelters. In the end the staff collected all the plates and we dined out there. I still laugh at the time when one class mistook the noise of a sanding machine on a new floor for our alarm rattle and went to the shelters with the whole school following!

Like Ronald Molyneux, Miss Barrow particularly remembered the devastation in the morning after a raid:

We'd probably have to cycle to school through broken glass. I used to let the children lie on the gym floor and sleep after an all night raid; and I remember one child saying politely that she'd been hit by a bit of shrapnel and need she do anything on her back during the (gym) lesson. How they all took it in their stride.

Miss Barrow
1939

Miss Barrow, QM's Gym teacher, was impressed by the stoicism of the children.

Joan Walker, née Stanley (QM 1937-1944), although a pupil during the same period as Muriel Love, remembers the return to Liverpool better than the time in Shrewsbury. She remarks:

We must have been one of the most austere schools in the country (in wartime) with our raw unpainted walls and the grounds totally untended. I can remember being very cold, too, during times of fuel shortage, so that from time to time the whole school had to dash round the corridors, to keep up circulation. However, looking back, I am surprise at how little we war-time students missed, for we were introduced to opera, ballet and plays when the staff organised theatre outings, to Youth Hostelling in Wales and camping and pea-picking in Bickerstaffe.

Joan's experience of wartime secondary schooling contrasts with Bernard Browne's regrets at missing a great deal, and it is clear that schools varied greatly. They were only being able to provide a semblance of normality under difficult wartime conditions, as at Queen Mary, through the good will and determination of their staff. Schools for boys must have suffered more in this respect from young and energetic staff being called up to the Services.

At the beginning of the war, Muriel Wrench was a pupil at Waterloo Park School for Girls. Her memory of wartime schooldays in Liverpool makes it clear that even when schools were open, the children may well have been too tired to benefit greatly from their lessons:

We had a lot of raids. One night we had to leave home because of an unexploded bomb. With neighbours, we were sent to the church hall at Five Lamps, Waterloo. It was scary, walking along Crosby Road with the Ack Ack guns firing and, because it was moonlight, seeing the German planes. The hall was very full and Mum and Mrs Davies thought it would be dangerous there if a bomb fell on the hall, so we walked on to St John's Road to beg safety with Mrs Davies' friends, and we stayed until morning, when we schoolgirls were packed off to school as if it was an ordinary day. However much we had been up in the night, it was always 'Sorry, love, can't leave you any longer, you'll be late for school – up you get!'

It must have been impossible for schools to maintain any reliable information about their pupil's whereabouts. Children might be in school one day and absent the next for so many reasons. Muriel remembers that after their home was destroyed, her parents decided not to live in Liverpool any longer:

I was amazed to be told that we were going to Prestatyn. Father's cousin, Ernest, had told my parents that if we were bombed out, we were to go to them – no need to ask – just go. So, packed into the side-car, Mother has to settle in with our worldly goods and I am on the pillion behind Dad. Just before we leave, I see a friend from school – I tell her that we are leaving and won't be coming back. I have since wondered whether she told the teachers at school or if they came to know.

Chapter Seven

Dangerous Games for Boys… and Girls

Although many schools had reopened a short time after the beginning of the war, they were often open for limited hours, perhaps morning or afternoon only. It was impossible for the authorities to keep track of children when some were evacuated, others were at home. There was also constant coming and going as children returned home and then, perhaps, went away again. This situation offered plenty of opportunities for freedom and adventure which some children, especially boys, were quick to appreciate.

Jim Williams, who had returned from evacuation for the winter of 1940, remarks on the difference in the experience of a child compared with the adult perception of events. Jim enjoyed a freedom that would have been unlikely in peacetime:

> Well, the war was getting a bit heated. My Dad was away at sea and the Battle of the Atlantic was at its height, but for me, it was great… 1940 saw some air raids but the May Blitz of 1941 was the worst thing I've experienced and I did seven years as a Naval Gunner and was in the Korean war, but this was something else… the city was destroyed, but us kids were out collecting shrapnel. And the schools were closed so we weren't too upset, but I can only imagine what the older people were going through. Well, anyway, we got on with life. Plenty of bombed houses to play in… a thing to remember was the Yanks coming over and us kids going down to the Pierhead to meet them and asking for chewing gum off them and they always obliged, so we were happy.

Peter McGuiness remembers that the morning after an air-raid:

> It was very exciting for young children, boys, in particular, to look for shrapnel and to take a large piece into school gave considerable kudos. My school was bombed, but to me this just meant an extra holiday. From time to time I saw a lot of bombed houses, but I do not remember seeing anyone injured.

Lawrence Whittaker was only six in 1941. Nevertheless, like most boys, he was keen to find some shrapnel or other souvenirs:

> One day, I found a bullet, only about half an inch long and put it in my pocket to gloat over it later. In those days, it was backyard lavatories and when I was down there later in the day, I brought the bullet out of my pocket and was looking at it – it looked like a liquorice torpedo and I put it in my mouth and accidentally swallowed it! I didn't tell anyone as I thought I might get into more trouble or even get a good hiding for doing it! I never saw it again!

In Wavertree, Peter Robinson recalls:

> ...picking up shrapnel after a raid and it was still warm – we played in bombed houses and shops, always chased by the wardens. We never knew what danger was – just fun in those days – we loved the black-out. There were big Emergency Water Supply tanks – quite big – brick-built for the Fire Service to use during raids. Again, dangerous! But in summer, they were swimming pools and in winter, skating rinks!

In Anfield, Alan Bentley also remembers the additional excitement afforded by the storage of wartime equipment:

> My friends and I used to play in the grounds around Liverpool Football Club. It was a child's paradise. It was full of lifeboats, as well as huge amounts of timber stowed on top of each other. We enjoyed playing hide-and-seek. Also, on the Kop side, facing Walton Breck Road, there was a steep bank, down which we would slide on the seat of our pants. It was such fun!

One can imagine that mothers dealing with clothes rationing were not so delighted!

Geoff Halligan was very young at the beginning of the war, two in October 1939, and he lived in Rosslyn Avenue, Maghull, an area that was considered safe enough to receive evacuees. Nevertheless, this is one of Geoff's earliest memories:

> The wail of the air raid siren and the drone of bombers overhead prompted a hasty scramble down the stairs and into a huddle under the sturdy dining table. One or two nearby explosions shook the house. An incendiary bomb bounced off the roof and blazed fiercely in the garden, lighting up the whole area, much to the consternation of the local ARP warden. My Dad, clad only in his 'long-johns' feverishly worked at the stirrup pump. I still have the tail-fin of that errant fire-stick.

When Irene Collinson's brothers returned home from Wales, 'they collected schrapnel, which Brian tried to flatten out in the mangle, and Billy turned the handle. It nearly took the top of Brian's thumb!' But Irene herself, who came home from Wales as a fourteen-year-old school leaver, was older than both her brothers and more aware of the danger of war. Her home was a cottage near the Bootle municipal golf course, which her father had helped to construct. This was taken over for anti-aircraft guns and the family had been issued with earplugs because of the noise:

> When I came home I worked in a hotel in Liverpool with my mother. The guns were still on the golf course, so sometimes we slept at the hotel. The (enemy) planes were trying to bomb the guns so our house wasn't safe. One night a big oil ship at the docks was bombed... everywhere was lit up as if it was daylight, but it was four in the morning. We went back to our cottage but it was cordoned off, so an ARP warden took us all to his house... the all clear went... then the siren went again and the lady, his wife, put us children under the table with all the cushions on top of it to keep us safe. I'm seventy-eight and I remember every awful minute of it.

Arthur Williams had a brother who was two years older than him and 'one of their hobbies was to collect pieces of bombs... our main hobby was to swap them at school'. The explosion of the ammunition train at Clubmoor, remembered by Arthur Williams who was evacuated to Colomendy Camp because of this devastating event, happened on the night of 3 May 1941. Even for those times, it was a very dramatic event that made a lasting impression on those who were anywhere near it.

My father-in-law, Frank Russell, serving in the Fire Service, was there that night, in great danger of losing his life. The scene was like a massive firework display as the ammunition started to explode, one truck taking fire from the next and then exploding, while the firemen were trying to extinguish the flames to stop them spreading. There was bomb damage to houses and other buildings that had been rocked by the blast several miles away. Added to the surreal nature of the event was the gun-cotton, drifting to the ground for miles around, giving the effect of a snow-fall. A number of firemen were amongst the casualties that night. Frank's reappearance at home, covered in gun cotton, brought the comment from my brother-in-law, Harold, then aged three 'Oh, look, Daddy is a snowman!

The innocent unawareness of danger in very young children, as displayed by Harold, was also apparent in older children for whom a spirit of adventure and childish curiosity often outweighed caution.

William (Bill) Courtliff, aged eleven in 1939, lived in Walton, and has vivid memories of the explosion of the ammunition train, including the gun cotton draping the trees along Queens Drive and the whole area. Bill recalls:

> We lived in Cherry Lane and when the Blitz was at its height, we used to go straight to bed in the air raid shelter in the garden, without bothering to settle in the house, as we knew we would only be disturbed later. On the night of the ammunition train explosion, the burning train passed along the railway line behind our house, but we were completely unaware of it. Later, after the All-Clear had been sounded and we were back in the house, we could hear the terrific explosions happening for some time afterwards. Next morning all the local lads went along to see what could be seen and, hopefully, to collect some souvenirs. Shrapnel was highly prized, but the nose of a shell-case was even better, because it had the numbers and rings for the settings on it. The morning after the explosion of the ammunition train, there were bombs and shells lying around everywhere – some of them still live, although we didn't know that! Kids were kicking them around and standing on the circular ones, balancing and rolling along, like people in the circus!

Bernard Browne remembers some of the damage caused to properties in Clubmoor and the surrounding district:

> With Grandmother living with us on a permanent basis, we needed more room and went from a 'kitchen-house' to a 'parlour-house' in Gatcliff Road, close to Larkhill Park. Being in Clubmoor, close to the railway sidings, the house had received some damage when the ammunition train exploded. To start with, we could not use the

Harold and Frank Russell in the garden in Farrer Street, Clubmoor, with taped windows and a vegetable plot in the background. Harold is wearing a tin hat.

front door and had to use the back door to go in and out. But with all the destruction and damage there was no other vacant property. After a while, council workmen repaired the front door. From my point of view, Clubmoor was much nearer school at St Edward's and I could cycle there and even come home for my lunch.

Brenda Bryce's father was a crane driver on the Gladstone Docks, a skilled reserved occupation. She recalls him returning home from another explosion; this one was in the docks:

I remember one night Dad came home from work, as usual up the 'jigger' – I opened the back door to the knock and almost died of fright when this ghost confronted me! It was Dad covered in white latex foam rubber from a ship that was blown up by one of Adolf's pals. Dad was totally covered in white rubber. I don't remember how Mum got if off him! Memories!

Albert Lewis, from Bullens Terrace in Bootle, remembers that:

In common with other friends, I climbed drainpipes to many roofs to collect shrapnel which we would swap for larger and better pieces (the boys' thing of that age). We, five of us, looked forward to meeting in our front garden air raid shelter escape hatch where we found that using a candle and covering it with an upturned old enamel washing up bowl with holes in it, provided us with light and heat in the cold winter nights.

But as well as enjoying some boyish adventures with his mates, like some other young children in wartime, Albert came up against the stark realities of conflict:

The empty desks at school the next morning, following an air raid, told their own story and I never saw some of my school friends again. I observed an apparently headless body, covered by a blanket, being carried on a stretcher, its outline was clear.

Despite the immediacy of the horror and danger, Albert wanted to 'do his bit'. He remembers that:

I ruined a brand new pair of shoes helping the firemen at a large fire – fetching cups of tea etc. in the Marsh Lane Rail Coal Depot, very much to the annoyance of my mother... I also helped a policeman, when he had to go away for a short time to attend to other matters, to stop people going into an area where an unexploded bomb had been found.

Gordon Crompton was five in 1939 and lived in Aigburth, but remembers that when the bombing started in 1940 it seemed like the 'war really started':

My first memorable experience came one evening – I was upstairs getting ready for bed when the air raid siren started and I dashed into my parents bedroom, where my kid sister, aged four, was being prepared for bed – I was very frightened not having much clue as to what was happening... I heard the drone of the aircraft and then the eerie sound of bombs whistling through the air. My mother suddenly cried out 'Duck, this one is for us!' and pushed us onto the floor. Within a second there was a massive explosion, luckily it didn't hit our house but damaged three houses only approximately a hundred yards down the road. Fortunately, no-one was killed.

This was obviously a very frightening experience, but, typically of children at that time, it did not take long for Gordon and his friends to make the best of the situation:

Out of tragedy can come good, this being the case with us kids, because the site was cleared rather quickly as the road led to St Michael's railway station. This land provided a marvellous playground for us kids and, what made it more exciting, a huge mound of debris was created and the authorities covered it with layers of soil. This became our mountain.

Gordon goes on to say:

Neither my sister or I was evacuated, and this was the norm for the south of Liverpool (except for those living in close proximity to Garston Docks) because all the large ships were docked in the north end of Liverpool, except for the oil and coal installations at the Dingle and Herculaneum Docks.

There were children evacuated from all parts of the city, but Gordon's adventures clearly indicate that there were many children about in his neighbourhood:

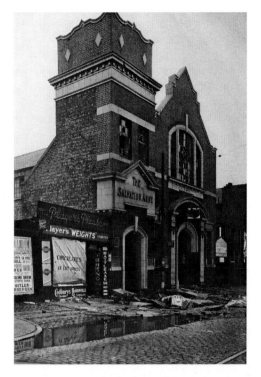

Damage to the Salvation Army Hall, Bootle. A poster on the shop nextdoor labels Hitler 'the Beast of Berlin'.

I was out as soon as my mother would allow me in the mornings after a raid, collecting shrapnel, because even when no bombs dropped in our area, flak from gunfire or parts falling off German bombers returning home were scattered everywhere. I don't know what happened to all this shrapnel, because no-one I know has any and I have a suspicion that the powers-that-be instructed our parents to hand in the shrapnel so that more weapons could be made!

I remember the building of a round Emergency Water Supply tank on waste land near St Michael's school. We kids had a wonderful time playing ducks and drakes, throwing wood into the water and then betting each other who could hit it first with a stone, and there were plenty of those hanging around. The most popular game was trying to throw a stone from one side of the tank to the other. Just across the road from the tank, a car was parked... it wasn't too long before it became a wreck. You should have seen it after five years, because we kids used to have a marvellous time playing in it and no-one chastised us ever.

Gordon especially remembers one dramatic incident:

It was towards the end of the war on a late afternoon – I was in the outside toilet during a thunderstorm with the door slightly open when I witnessed the most amazing sight. I noticed a barrage balloon, not doing much, when suddenly a streak of lightning hit it and it blew up and descended to earth in a million or more pieces. What a sight for sore eyes!

In the *Daily Post* of 1 May 1940, a letter from W.A. Swift, the vicar of St Cleopas, Toxteth, voices his dismay at the lawlessness of children running wild and causing damage in his parish. He suggests that 'a return to the use of the birch is urgently called for'. A week later, in the *Daily Post* of 8 May, a letter from 'A Social Worker' responds by reporting an incident when she visited the home of a nine-year-old girl seen 'lorry-hanging' – a dangerous game involving hanging onto the back of a lorry and getting an illicit ride. The girl at first denied the accusation, but, confronted by her mother, she confessed and received immediate retribution in the form of 'a proper spanking', after which she was obliged to apologise. The social worker concludes her letter with the belief that many parents were unaware of their children's activities and that if they were informed, 'The present wave of naughtiness could be spanked out of existence in quite a short time.'

Ralph Pedersen, living in the centre of Liverpool, and six in 1941, remembers, 'Boys in Pitt Street were kicking bombs away from houses before they exploded and so prevented fires.' He also brings to life the photographs of the war-torn city of Liverpool that later generations have seen:

> When you see photographs of the Lord Street area after the bombing, you see a scene of devastation, piles of rubble and tortured steel – a scene devoid of life – this, however, was the icing on the cake, below which cellars which could be entered. Our group of boys, like rats, would scramble through the mountain of shattered concrete to the basement stairs and to a lake that had invaded the whole of the basement area. Light filtered through various holes and in the dim light, we built rafts with timber that was lying everywhere and went rafting through the underworld.

Boys who remained in Liverpool often banded together in informal groups of friends to explore the strange world of a city at war. There was a great deal of status attached to collections of shrapnel and other assorted objects, but also to acts of bravado. None of the boys wanted to lose face. Most of the authority figures, such as fathers and teachers, were either away on war service or evacuated with other children. Indeed, for some children, it was the difference at school when some of the teachers were called up, that had been the first of many changes in their lives. Older men and married women had returned to teaching, but it was impossible to keep track of all the children. Some children were away; others had returned but the school authorities were not aware that they were back in Liverpool. Mothers were sometimes struggling to cope with the difficulties of damaged homes, queuing for rations, constant worry and sleeplessness and, often, younger children.

Phil Taylor's memories illustrate this situation:

> Where we lived in Liverpool was not far from the docks and whole streets had been bombed. Our house was not bombed but all the glass windows were blown out. In our street, there were three big air raid shelters made out of brick and concrete. There was nothing inside, so, when the sirens wailed, everyone in the street, which was mostly women and children, because all our Dads were away fighting in the war, took blankets and pillows and chairs to sit on. And that was where we spent the night. When the All Clear went, usually not until morning, we boys were the first out of the shelter to see what had happened and then we would go looking for shrapnel. Sometimes a cry would go up that they were digging bodies out of a street that had been directly hit with bombs and we boys would race to watch the grisly finds. Somehow, we did not feel anything, just interest.

Phil points out that this group of boys rarely went to school.

> We would be in bombed houses looking for shrapnel and pushing houses down. Yes, it sounds unbelievable now, but a row of houses could be bombed and shells, just the walls, left standing. They were so unstable that if a few boys at one end pushed, the whole row of existing walls fell down like a pack of cards. We were always covered with plaster and soot. How our Mums kept us clean I never knew.

Bill Backshall, in Litherland, also remembers being attracted to danger:

> One Christmas, a heavy raid developed over three or four nights, with a substantial amount of damage being caused by high explosives, incendiary and oil bombs, the latter two creating some fierce fires. I was inquisitive and foolishly attracted to some of these large fires, so, with a chum, I ran down to Seaforth where a great blaze was reflected against the sky. Following the glow, we found Rushes timber yard was well ablaze, sending up volumes of smoke, flames and crackling sparks a hundred and fifty feet up into the night sky. The regular and auxiliary firemen were desperately trying to control it. I met my brother, Chay, who had also been attracted to the fire and he told me that our brother-in-law, Jimmy Tracey, an auxiliary fireman was around fighting the flames. Sadly, Jimmy was badly hurt during an incident that night.
>
> Roaring and crackling flames, the noise of the falling bombs and the continual barrage of anti-aircraft fire made hearing difficult, but still, above the din, we spotted a wee reddish-silver plane swooping above us, spraying the scene with machine-gun fire, just to add to the firemen's other hazards. It didn't take long for Sammy and myself to withdraw and leave the scene to the brave firemen, policemen and wardens.

Boys were constantly trying to find a piece of shrapnel or some other object that would give them greater status in the playground, despite the fact that children were equally constantly discouraged from picking up unidentified objects by dire warnings of the consequences. David Buckley remembers that:

> Each morning after the raids, I and my friend would go around the streets looking for shrapnel, to see who could find the biggest piece. But we were warned not to pick up anything else as the Germans used to drop what looked like fountain pens, and if you picked one up, it would explode and blow your hand off.

David also:

> … acquired an incendiary bomb without the fins, as a swap from a friend , which had been dropped and had not gone off, probably falling on soft ground and being a silly young lad I decided that I would unscrew the front part to see what was inside. When I got it open, I found that it contained a lot of black powder which I put in the upturned lid of Mum's metal bin in the back yard. I decided that I would throw a lighted match into it to see if it would burn, and, boy, did it go… the flames shot up about ten feet high and when it had gone out, I saw my Mum's bin lid had been ruined; what a telling off I got for that.

The 'telling off' was almost certainly related more to his mother's horror at what might have happened to her son than to the loss of a dustbin lid for the duration!

Alan Parks, born in 1935 and living in Crosby, was similarly inquisitive about his finds:

> Bomb disposal men would visit school, Forefield Junior School, and show us examples of munitions we might find that could cause injury, but this did not quell my curiosity when I found a blank cartridge that I now know to be a .303 calibre. This I placed in the vice with the blank end pointing downwards so that I could point a nail where the pin would normally strike. I hit the nail with a hammer and it fired. My toes escaped mutilation!

Ron Rigby, in Lydiate, remembers an evacuee at the village school called John. Like Alan, John found an unfired .303 shell:

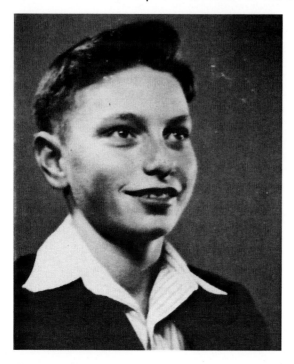

Ron Rigby, aged ten.

We were constantly being warned about picking up war debris of any sort, but John decided to fire this shell. He put it in a crevice in the wall in the school playground and hit the firing cap smartly with a nail in a piece of wood. The bullet could go nowhere, so the casing flew backwards, grazing John's head and leaving a hairless streak.

Howard Croston, born in 1933, was another boy with a shrapnel collection. He was the youngest of eight children and lived in the Custom House, a public house in Duke Street in the centre of the city, an area that was under heavy enemy fire. He remembers:

Many a time were we caught in the bath when the sirens sounded. We had to run to the air raid shelter in Ayrton-Saunders basement (a chemical warehouse) with a blanket wrapped around us. Sometimes after an air-raid, the following morning, my brother and I would go out into Duke Street and the surrounding areas to collect shrapnel and other items. I had a Mickey Mouse bucket and spade. Sometimes the shrapnel was too hot to pick up.

The choice of the basement of a chemical warehouse for an air-raid shelter seems a strange one. The resultant conflagration had a bomb fallen on the building would have been frightening!

Sometimes, there were other advantages to be had from being daring! Arthur Graham remembers children foraging for food and for items to sell. Arthur was eight years old when he was evacuated along with his brothers, Billy and Tommy, to a house called Eastfield, in Meols Drive, Hoylake, where there were a number of other children from Liverpool and Birkenhead and also a girl from France:

It was a 'managed' house – WVS? Council? We were always hungry and would raid the larder for anything edible. The cheese was always green, but we ate it. Being hungry, orchards were our delight; turnips out of the field went down well. The older boys would go along the railway lines, knocking the wooden wedges that held the lines in place and sell them for firewood, maybe one every eight sleepers. I can always remember them crawling through the barbed wire of the mine-fields alongside Hoylake Municipal Golf Course. They chased me away. I was looking at the mines and the trip wires. They were collecting golf balls to sell on.

Arthur looks back on those days and, despite feeling hungry, comments, 'I enjoyed every minute as an evacuee!'

It was not just the boys who were so daring that they were in danger. Girls also had their collections of shrapnel and took part in adventures that would not have met with their parents' approval. Enid Johnston was six years old when war began. She recalls:

We used to go round after the air raids to collect shrapnel – girls as well as boys! I well remember the night that Lewis's was bombed, and the next day, people were finding bits of fur coats as there must have been a strong wind. I lived then in Allerton, and our house backed onto the main railway line from Lime Street to Euston, London, and so there were many troop trains going through. We used to stand on the railings at the bottom of the railway embankment and watch and wave to the soldiers. We must have looked like 'The Railway Children' and we particularly liked it when the trains were carrying American troops, as they must have been sorry for us, and always used to throw chocolate and chewing gum and sweets to us. We were forbidden to go on the railway embankment, and we were too frightened anyway, but when these 'goodies' were thrown to us, we had to, but it was just straight over and back.

Another railway experience is remembered by Jean Campbell:

I remember Liverpool burning. You could see the flames from the bombing. I remember sitting under the table under the stairs in our little two-up two-down terrace house listening to the bombs falling. When it got too bad, we would all go into the brick shelter that had been built in the road. It was damp and smelt horrible. I remember going to Edge Hill railway lines after it had been bombed and finding wine gums, all burnt. We ate them.

Even children who had been evacuated were not always safe. Vic Smith, happily settled in Bagillt, remarks:

As far as being in danger from bombs, I was near to danger in Bagillt when a bomb fell on a local farm, killing a school friend and his mother. This obviously brought home the horror of war, but, in other ways, the war provided many exciting experiences such as the time a German plane was shot down on the Dee estuary about a mile away – I was frustrated that I wasn't allowed to get close enough. Another experience was being in the fields with Italian prisoners-of-war, who were working with only a couple of guards.

Like Bill Backshall, other children did not always take cover when they should have done. Brenda Bryce, living in Walton, remembers:

We kids used to try to spot the 'Kraut' planes – we learnt the sound of their engines. There would be cries of 'Kraut! Kraut!' (our name for Germans) from us kids. Silly little idiots – but we had no fear of them. We used to stand and cheer the Spitfires – our guys.

Chapter Eight

Make Do and Mend

Enid Johnston remembers:

Nothing was wasted during the war. Jumpers were painstakingly unpicked and the good wool was mixed with other bits to make new jumpers. There were lots of striped and Fair-isle jumpers around. Coats were sometimes made from blankets, or one would be made from the good parts of two others, and it was not unusual to see a coat with a different coloured top and skirt, or maybe a yoke and sleeves would be different. If anyone was lucky enough to come by some parachute silk (usually on the black market) it was turned into lovely underwear (which must have been very hot) and even wedding dresses. Wedding dresses were borrowed a lot – sometimes at least four brides would wear the same dress.

Enid's school in Allerton was organising salvage collection, 'We had to take salvage into school to help the war effort – there were large hessian sacks hanging in the cloakroom for waste paper, cans etc.' All the family were involved, 'My grandmother had iron railings taken from outside her house and all the park railings also went to be melted down. People also gave surplus pots and pans.' As the war went on for six long years, and it became very difficult to buy pots and pans, there must have been some housewives who, perhaps, privately regretted their patriotic generosity.

Bones, paper and rubber were also collected and there were special pages in magazines, such as *Good Housekeeping*, involving mothers and children and encouraging them to work together to be 'salvage-minded'.

Shirley Landrum remembers that her school in Roby also organised salvage collection:

Once a week we had to take a bit of scrap cardboard called 'salvage' to school to help with the war effort. I never knew how it helped and we could not ask questions; that would be being cheeky. Some people today think that re-cycling is a new skill. For us, it was second nature. 'Waste not, want not' was our motto. Garments were unravelled; the wool was held over steam to get rid of the wrinkles and re-knitted. Coats were cut down; sheets were turned sides-to-middle and I had a kilt made form a pre-war rug and a dressing gown out of an army blanket. Grey, of course! It was mostly a black and white world then.

Margaret Barber, living with her aunt, remembers that she and her brother and sisters were:

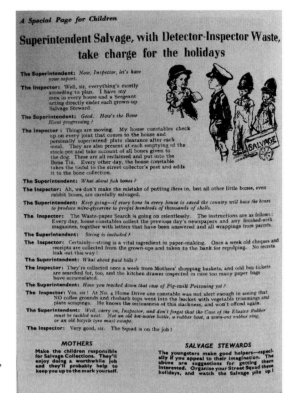

'A Special Page for Children', *Good Housekeeping* magazine, 1943, encourages children to form Salvage Squads.

Little girl knitting 'Comforts for the Troops', *Good Housekeeping*, February 1943.

… taught care with money, which was very short, never to owe a penny or to waste anything. We all learnt to recycle the hard way. We learnt to sew and knit and we knitted balaclavas, socks, gloves and scarves. I made a good skirt that lasted for years from my father's grey flannels.

Like most of her generation, Joan Gillett's mother was skilful at knitting and sewing:

I remember Mum having a sewing machine and making dresses for my sister and me from old dresses of hers. She also did a lot of knitting to help out with the clothes coupons.

Joan Tisdale, eleven when the war began, 'read all the advice on how to Make Do and Mend in the *Echo* and on radio.' In this way, she learnt:

… how to make a siren suit for a child from an adult coat. I was only thirteen by this time and I had a little nephew, two years old. I made this suit by hand and my nephew was very happy with his 'Winston Churchill Siren Suit'.

Another child who had a siren suit was Olive Woods, who remembers 'getting woken up in the middle of the night to put on a siren suit with a zip up the front.' Olive was also 'doing her bit' by 'knitting blankets at school for the needy, although I must say, we were all needy in those days!'

Betty Harrison, evacuated to her Lake District relations, learnt to knit and to make 'peg' rugs. Back home in Mossley Hill, after the cellar of the family home was reinforced, Betty's mother was equally resourceful, 'My mother needed some new curtains, which she dyed and made from flour bags, or rather, sacks as we bought flour by the hundredweight then.'
    Like John Johnson and the Boy Scouts, the Girl Guides were also involved in useful wartime activities. Joyce Jones was a Guide. She remembers that they were issued with grey or khaki wool to knit for the Forces:

I made gloves, scarves and stockings; we sometimes put our names and addresses in the toes of the stockings and I got a letter from a sailor who had received a pair. His ship was later torpedoed and he drowned.

Joyce was also involved in her local church and remembers that 'the church collected clothes in case of people being bombed out and they actually came in handy when an ammunition train was bombed… houses were badly damaged and the people stayed at the church.' Most of Joyce's teenage years were in wartime. She started work in 1941, aged fourteen, in the local sub-Post Office. Like many girls of her generation, she was skilful at sewing, knitting, embroidery and crochet. She remembers how bed linen was made to last as long as possible, 'When sheets became thin, they were cut down the middle and the two ends sewn together and the thin part hemmed.' This meant that the thin areas were tucked in at the sides of the bed and the newer material was in the centre.
    Joyce continues:

We all had handed down clothes, and knitted things which had gone too big or the elbows gone out of jumpers or cardigans, they were unpicked and knitted, maybe with two colours, or made into gloves, socks or hats. Everything was 'Make Do and Mend'. We made rugs out of old clothes that weren't able to be made into something; they were cut into strips and threaded into sacking. We also crocheted blankets out of odd wool and used them in the shelter. There were no toys in the shops, and you could buy a type of wool, used for fishermen's long stockings, free of coupons, so I bought some and knitted dogs with it, (doubled and looped), stuffing them, for the Christmas Fair and they were snapped up. It was surprising the things people came up with. I made a dress at school which was worn Sundays and during the week I had a gymslip with a white blouse (washed every night to wear the next day) or a jumper knitted by myself, with either wool three-quarter socks, long black wool stockings or ankle socks. One pair of shoes. Sometimes we used to manage to get flour bags, which were opened up and bleached. We made cushion covers, table runners and mats and embroidered them, sometimes, if there were enough, curtains could be made but these were usually dyed. Father's old trousers were made into skirts and even old hats were remodelled. Very few things were ever thrown away. Some people got pieces of parachute material and made underwear. I made a golliwog out of an old black stocking for a Guide badge; this was given to a little girl. Old toys were passed from one family to another.

The golliwog was an unremarkable nursery toy in the 1940s and had the advantage of being easily made at home, unlike the teddy-bear, which required furry material that could not be obtained. People were wearing old fur coats, and old garments with fur collars. An old sock was more readily available.

Like Joyce, Evelyn Davies left school during the war. Her first job was in the Post Office at Brighton-le-Sands, near Waterloo. 'I certainly needed my times tables for that job!'

Later, she took a job with the solicitor, Marcus Davies, in Dale Street, Liverpool. Clothes were a problem for all those growing up during the war years and Evelyn was no exception:

At that time, clothes and shoes were still scarce and I needed new foot-wear. I had to order the only ones available – a pair of clogs, and then waited months for them. The uppers were of navy blue leather with red laces, but I think the soles and heels must have been wood! I wore them to go to work and every step I took resounded loudly as I walked round the office. Marcus Davies would say 'I hear Miss Courtman is wearing her clogs today.' So I tried not to wear them too often. Yes, being a teenager in wartime was very different to now, another story.

Elva Barooah, still only nine when the war ended, also remembers that rationing caused problems with foot-wear:

Evelyn Davies (right) in her first job, aged fourteen, at Brighton le Sands Post Office, near Waterloo.

Clothes didn't mean much to me, but my shoes caused trouble – either because we were poor or because of the rationing. My shoes were very hard and I always got blisters on my heels with a new pair. My father did mend our shoes, using a last, but often they leaked; we had cardboard insoles put in but still often had soaking socks and wet feet.

Elva also recalls other shortages:

The only heating in the house was a coal fire in the 'kitchen' – the main living room – This also heated the water. The other rooms were freezing. Once, my mother and father went out with our old pram to get some coal from somewhere. When they got back, exhausted, I had let the fire go out, as I'd been reading. That meant trouble and I did feel guilty. I remember that the kitchen had red and blue tiles directly on the earth floor; the other rooms mainly had lino. There was a carpet in the front room and my mother and father made hearth rugs from scraps of material.

Sister and brother, Joan and Jim MacMurtry, born in 1938 and 1942 respectively, remember their resourceful parents. Jim recalls, 'All clothing was rationed and money wasn't plentiful, so handmade clothes were the order of the day. Mum was a great knitter!' Joan remembers:

Because Dad had time on his hands at sea, he used to make most of our toys. A fort or scooter for my brother: a doll's house, sweetshop or bookcase for me. Dad also used his time at sea to make those rag rugs. No fitted carpet since has had quite the same excitement as a new coloured mat on the tiled floor.

Geoff Halligan's father is described by his son as 'a most inventive and skilled Dad.' Geoff remembers:

With toys and children's activities at a premium, inventiveness was the name of the game. Most intriguing of all were the toys that appeared at Christmas and Birthday times. A wooden Liverpool Standard Tram with sprung trolley arm; a Wellington Bomber with spinning props and landing gear; articulated timber trucks (just like the ones in the timber fields) and ump-teen other delights made of scrap wood from soap boxes and the like. The 'pièce de résistance', however, was a pedal LMS steam engine 2270 created lovingly by my Dad for me from an old oil drum, some scrap wood, four old pram wheels and an ingeniously created set of controls. It was pedalled for many miles and was the envy of all the kids in the road who clambered for rides in the converted soap box truck that coupled up behind!

Geoff continues, 'The engine waits for me to restore it – perhaps I will one day as a testa-ment to the inventive love of parents who brought me up through the war. I was kept safe and was certainly never bored.' The photograph shows Geoff outside his house, at the controls of his engine with an air-raid shelter in the grass verge in front of the last house on the opposite side of the road.

Like Geoff's Wellington Bomber, many toys had a wartime flavour. A knitting pattern of the time shows how to 'Knit your own Servicewoman' from scraps of wool that could be spared. It includes patterns for a Wren, a WAAF and an ATS girl. Many little girls who had such dolls would have had older sisters, cousins or aunts in the services, and no doubt, their dolls were named appropriately.

A photograph of Harold Russell in the garden of Farrer Street shows his wooden toy tank, and in the background the criss-cross taped windows. Harold was only two or three when this photograph was taken; he says, 'I'm not sure whether the tank was made by my

Geoff Halligan with his steam engine, made from scraps by his father, in Rosslyn Avenue, Maghull. On the left is a street shelter, marked with a white 'H'.

Harold Russell with a homemade toy wooden tank.

Dad, but it probably was, because I remember him making other small toys and tools when I was a little older.'

Harold also remembers:

I had whooping cough when I was about six; I was ill in bed for about nine weeks. During this period, I had sometimes to be left alone while Mum did some shopping. Once she brought me back some small paints and a paint brush as a reward for being a good boy and staying in bed until she came back. The paints were small amounts, all different colours, in metal bottle tops or 'jinks' as they were called.

Proper boxes of paints were not being produced at this time, but some ingenious person must have produced these tiny paints to amuse artistic children.

Despite living in Halsall, Frank Holcroft's home was:

> … virtually destroyed when a returning aircraft jettisoned its remaining bombs on our cottage in the middle of nowhere. There were no windows left, the stairs were blown away and about a foot of rubble everywhere, yet we were nice and safe under our strong old table.

Despite this experience, one of Frank's memories is of Christmas:

> As times were hard, Dad used to make our toys. We could always tell when Father Christmas was due, as we could always smell the fresh paint. One year, in particular, he made me a wooden steam engine and threshing machine. He told me in later years that it was once the garden gate.

Alan Bentley, three in 1939, remembers:

> My father served in the King's Own Regiment. On occasions, when he was on leave, he would make wooden toys for my sister and me. I remember having a toy fort, with a draw-bridge, whilst he made two wooden prams for my sister, Joan, and our cousin, Kath.

Not all fathers were able to make toys and many were away in the Forces. Shirley Landrum's father was in the Fire Service so he did not have much spare time, but she says:

> I remember watching my Dad and Uncle making and painting wooden toys and later feeling very special when I saw them in a shop window in Huyton. Toys were not easy to get and these sold well. They were bright red engines and yellow pull-along ducks on green wheels.

Children also learned to 'make do' and to be creative with few toys. They also learned to make their own toys and, of course, the act of creating playthings became a pastime in its own right.

Shirley remembers:

> My sister and I had few toys but a lot of time and imagination. We did a lot of drawing on scrap paper, circuses, bus queues and self-portraits. We also worked out knitting patterns and made cardigans for our few dolls. In good weather, we played out, making 'houses' in the bushes and trees and mixing mud for pies in a hollow in the base of one tree. They were left to dry in tin lids and gently tipped out before being 'eaten' – just pretend!

Enid Johnston remembers how inventive and creative people could be:

> People used to make their own jewellery. We would collect cockle shells, and when scrubbed, someone would carefully drill holes in them and we would thread them onto a cord, and paint them. I had one with my name on.

Joan and Jim McMurtry remember how determined the adults were that children should have as much fun as was possible under wartime conditions, so the very activities caused by having to 'Make Do and Mend' became part of the pleasure. They had their toys at Christmas made by their father. But they also have other happy memories. Joan says:

A boy making a model warship, *Good Housekeeping*, September 1943.

A girl with Christmas tree and wartime gifts, *Good Housekeeping* Christmas Issue, 1941.

At Christmas, we made our own decorations. By a happy coincidence, we had an aunt who served in a wallpaper shop. She used to bring us the cuttings and we made paper chains to go across the rooms. We loved the really bright, glittery ones. I later wondered what a whole room would have looked like with some of those samples!

Jim adds:

Christmas was happy. As children, we made paper decorations stuck together with flour and water. Milk bottle tops (cardboard to make wool bobbins and silver ones for tinsel) were saved up all year. Our Christmas stockings (pillowcases) usually contained an apple and a few sweets screwed up in paper and, maybe, a book, with perhaps one toy – a wooden fort for me – a sweetshop for my sister.

Shirley Landrum remembers her mother's efforts to create a pre-war-style Christmas stocking:

Christmas was a mixed blessing. Dolls were passed down from bigger cousins, but, secretly, Mum knitted coats, bonnets and bootees for them, to go in our stockings. There were crayons, a colouring book, a new penny, a handful of sweets and maybe a new book and an orange. The excitement was still there! In the dark we felt the bulk and tried to guess, then we had to wait until day-light to see if we were right.

Chapter Nine

Dig for Victory

As well as the rationing of clothes and fuel, food was also rationed and thrift was encouraged. Frances Jennings remembers Christmas 1940:

> Presents at Christmas were few; my parents would give me their coupons so that I could get a Selection Box. My mother managed to save dried fruit to make a bunloaf and Christmas Cake (no icing)… an extra ration of fresh meat was given. If you were lucky to get a Chicken or Turkey, then you were fortunate… a parcel from our relatives in America arrived with dresses for my mother and sisters, tobacco for my father and a doll for me, which had a broken arm sustained in travelling, but hopefully would be fixed in the Doll's Hospital, which was still open for a few days each week around Christmas time. There were very few toys, mainly second-hand. My Christmas parcel contained an apple, an orange, chocolate money, a skipping rope, a game of dominoes, a new school blouse and new shoes.

Shirley Landrum comments:

> I had a fairly mild war. Thousands died for the cause abroad; hundreds under the rubble of their own homes. No-one in my family died, for which I am grateful. But for a small girl, my hardships were real. Easter and Christmas were the worst. Being four years younger than me, Glenda had no memories of shopping in Woolworths for chocolate Easter Eggs, wrapped in shiny gold or silver paper and beautifully boxed, but I did. Mum got a recipe for eggs made out of soya flour, shaped and rolled in chocolate vermicelli (like hundreds and thousands). I pretended to like the awful things because she had tried so hard to make Easter special. She also boiled hen's eggs and put faces on them for us.

Special occasions, like weddings, were unlike those in pre-war days. The ban on iced cakes applied to wedding cakes, as well as Christmas and birthday cakes. Frances' sister married in 1941:

> On the wedding day, the air raid started at 7 p.m. during the celebrations. The wedding cake was an ordinary fruit cake with an imitation white cardboard cover, giving the appearance of icing. It was placed under a table because all the guests were ordered to go to a nearby park shelter, the raid was over by 4 a.m. On returning to my sister's in-laws' house, all the windows had been blown out and the wonderful wedding cake was covered in glass fragments, but the cardboard cover had saved the actual cake.

Morale was important. Just as children were being encouraged not to be 'doleful' and papers and magazines were encouraging them to be cheerful, so were they encouraged to take an active role in the activities of the Home Front. And in this war, children were also used to encourage high morale and to reinforce the messages that the government were trying to get across to the adult civilian population. Posters appeared, for instance, showing very small children reaching to put cabbage leaves into a waste-bin for pig food. David Buckley remembers that:

> On each end of the brick-built air raid shelters in the street, a metal bin was placed, and eve-ryone was asked to put their potato peelings, cabbage leaves, stale bread etc. in it. When they were full, they were taken away to make pig-swill.

Children were aware that there were things that could no longer be bought in the shops. Maureen Bentley, née Burrows, was told that:

> The Merchant Navy were very brave men, who risked their lives in sailing to other countries to bring things to Britain.' It was considered our duty to them and to our country to be as careful as we could with food and clothes and everything else. We never wasted a thing; every street had bins at the end for waste to feed the pigs with. Many people grew vegetables… and the older classes had hens, rabbits, an orchard and a vegetable patch at the back of the school.

This was in Southport. The Ministry of Agriculture issued 'Dig for Victory' leaflets. Number 23 'Making the Most of a Small Plot' gives a Plan and a Table of Planting for a small plot and suggests that:

> it will appeal specially to women and children, who may not be able to tackle a man-size plot… it shows how best to crop your small plot so that you get a few summer vegetables as well as health giving winter greens.

HM Stationery Office produced a Dig for Victory poster, reinforcing the notion that no child was too young to be involved in food production.

The expectation that children were expected not only to be thrifty with resources, but also to join in with the effort to produce more food, was reinforced by pictures in the newspapers of the Princesses, Elizabeth and Margaret Rose, with their gardening tools.

Help on the land was also needed to supplement the efforts of the Land Army in replac-ing the labour of the men who were in the Forces. Mavis Hardman, née Disley, joined in with the efforts of school camps through the Queen Mary High School, but many other schools were also involved. She remembers plenty of fun at Barrow Nook in Bickerstaffe, combined with a valuable contribution to the war effort:

> It was quite a common sight in the latter years of the war to see a farm lorry packed with schoolgirls jolting their way to pea-picking camp. It was at our allotted site that the Girl Guides in our midst came into their own, and while their experienced hands made short work of bell-tent erection, we lesser mortals found ourselves enveloped in canvas and guy-ropes… but, somehow, within a few hours, a most efficient-looking camp had mushroomed into existence, with our palliasses eventually filed with straw, and DDT scattered for the ben-efit of roving beetles.
>
> We were very slow and very clumsy picking our first hampers of peas, and I have a distinct recollection of one of our party shelling her peas until she was enlightened! But we must have improved; every year we paid our way and still managed to arrive home with a respectable

'Dig for Victory' poster, showing the
involvement of a very young child.

amount of pocket money. I remember long hot days when the sun and midges took their toll.
Then there were days when the ex-army groundsheets and ex-navy sou-westers proved their
worth. When it was our turn for the Friday night camp fire, we always invited our long-suffering
host, Farmer Rose and his family, to thank them for his kindness to us all. Usually one of the
Manchester Grammar schools conveniently held their boys' camp the same week, so they came
along too. Cocoa and buns provided a fitting close to a most enjoyable week, and it was not
solely patriotic fervour that made us all resolve to return the following year to Barrow Nook.

Mavis and her friends were fortunate in being allowed to keep some of their 'wages'. Doris
Jenkins, née Jost, one of the girls who went potato picking at Atcham during the period
of the school's evacuation, had a different experience, 'Alas! Miss Grayson decreed that this
was to be our war effort and the money was given to a war charity. We were not amused.'

But it was not just at camp or during evacuation that Queen Mary girls were 'Digging
for Victory'. The school was a raw new building in 1940 and although the school moved
in, the playing fields were still a future dream. Indeed, some school playing fields were
sacrificed for valuable food crops during the war. The QM site had large lawns at the front
of the building and two internal quadrangles. Pamela Booth, née Morton, recalled, '…the
quadrangles were planted with vegetables and salad produce. In the ground at the front
potatoes were grown and much to the delight of our mothers we were able to purchase
the crop when harvested.'

Pea-picking was also done by youngsters independent of adult organisation. Francis
(Nick) Nelson remembers, 'We picked peas in summer. Lads from school, which was
St Edward's in West Derby, used to get the Ribble bus out to the Weld Blundell pub in
Lydiate and we picked peas with Italian POWs at Allins Farm.'

Rationing began on the 8 January 1940. The first foods to be rationed were butter, sugar, bacon and ham. Later, other foods were also rationed. Meat was rationed from March 1940, by cost rather than weight, so a larger amount of a cheaper cut could be bought. Other items were rationed as the war progressed; these included cheese, jam, marmalade, treacle, cooking fats and tea. Tea leaves were used over and over again. The allowances of most of these goods fluctuated over the war years and some continued to be rationed afterwards. Bread was not rationed during the war, but it was rationed afterwards. This was resented by most people, who naturally expected things to improve in peacetime.

Despite the hardships and shortages of rationing, a great deal was done by the authorities to protect the health of the children of the nation. After 1942, children under five years old were entitled to subsidised orange juice, cod liver oil and milk from welfare clinics. When oranges were available, children under six years old were entitled to 1lb per week. Joan Gillett remembers visiting the clinic with her mother and baby sister, born in November 1942; she says, 'Another memory is of going to the clinic, off Carisbrooke Road, Kirkdale, to get bottles of orange juice and powdered baby milk in silver and blue tins. Babies were also weighed there.'

Free school milk was also available. Children under five had green ration books, entitling them to more of some items and less of others, such as tea. Children under six had some special allowances, such as oranges when these were available, but as shortages bit deeper, such luxuries became very rare. Older children up to age sixteen, and eighteen after 1944, had a blue ration book. The different colours denoted different ration entitlements. For instance, children with a green book received only half the meat allowance and no tea. The blue book meant an entitlement of three eggs per week, while adults hoped to get one. Eggs supplies fluctuated, so they were sometimes unavailable. Many people began to keep chickens, even in back yard runs. Children were also allowed about twice the amount of dried egg. Cheery posters with characters like Doctor Carrot, the children's best friend, and Potato Pete were introduced to encourage children to enjoy home-grown vegetables and adults to grow them, if at all possible.

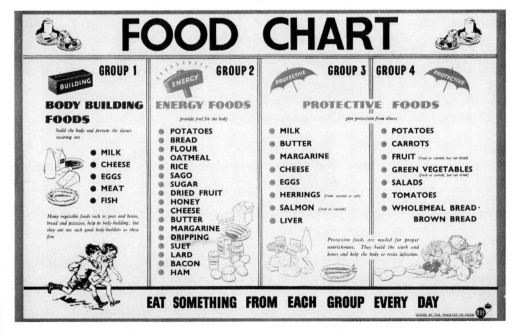

A food chart, showing rations in groups – 'Eat Something from Each Group Every Day.'

Doctor Carrot, the children's best friend.

A children's book in the 'Tuck Book' series was entitled *Happy Hours on the Food Front* and depicts a jolly family working to produce vegetables. The text makes sure to point out that Daddy is in the Home Guard.

Most people who had some garden began to grow their own vegetables, with encouragement from the government, who produced many leaflets and booklets to help them. Most suburban dwellers had their gardens down to lawn and flower beds, so food production was a new skill for them. Even people who were unaccustomed to gardening at all began to grow their own produce. My parents married during the war and my father, Alfred (Alf) Brown, took over a large garden in Maghull, after a childhood growing up in Everton, in houses with back yards. Books such as *The Vegetable Garden Displayed* (1943) and *A Garden Goes to War* (1940), both of which were on his bookshelves, were eagerly bought by people who wanted to produce nutritious and interesting additions to the family's rations. By 1945, around 75 per cent of the food eaten was being produced in Britain.

Some people also began to keep livestock in small gardens; hens were the most likely choice, with rabbits also kept as a food supply. Enid Johnston, who lived in Allerton, says:

> During the war, we kept hens in the back garden so we could have a supply of eggs as food rationing allowed only one egg per person per week. We had a very vicious, bad-tempered cockerel who we named 'Miss Banks' after our very bad-tempered head-mistress at school! If he ever managed to get out of the hen run (and he was quite good at this) he would run at us and go for our legs, and we were very frightened of him, and for this reason, we were never asked to collect the eggs.

Enid's father found a way to make up for the ground he had given up for the hen run and her mother found ways to make up for the loss of flowers for the house:

A Garden Goes to War, the cover shows a whole family involved in food production.

We had turned our garden – apart from the hen run – into a vegetable garden, as I think most people had to do if possible. My father also had an allotment to enable him to grow more and as we had no flowers to bring into the house, my mother would gather autumn leaves, greenery, seed-heads etc, to make some colour in the house. She also got some coloured wax from somewhere, and made small 'flowers' from the wax to put onto twigs.

In their wartime refuge in Prestatyn, Muriel Wrench's family settled down:

We made good use of the garden. My Grandma Eskrigge was a farmer's daughter, so Dad was keen on growing vegetables and fruit. Uncle Ernest kept hens and ducks. Also, being in the 'fridge business, Dad had contact with butchers and sometimes came home with extra meat.

Austin Gahan's parents both went out to work for the war effort, 'Poor Mum and Dad had to work such long hours; I had to stand in queues at the shops for food sometimes.' Despite their long working week, Austin's parents tried hard to provide a good and varied diet for their three children, 'As we had an allotment behind the gas-mask factory in Stopgate Lane, we would "Dig for Victory". My Dad also kept chickens in the back garden so we had plenty of eggs – giving any surplus eggs to our neighbours.'

Schools also provided filling dinners and nourishing drinks for children. And children understood that they must eat what was provided for them, and as they were hungry, there was little opportunity to be too fussy.

Nevertheless, children did not always enjoy eating what they were given and sometimes needed some encouragement. Muriel Wrench, at Rhyl High School, remembers:

School dinners were the norm and there was a lot of moaning – I, for one, never want to eat a butter bean again. I can see the History master, Mr Horton, grey hair, moustache and suit, standing at the Staff table, eating a bowl of tapioca pudding to prove it was edible and looking as if he had a smell under his nose. If we hadn't been such well brought-up pupils, I think we would have rioted; but the poor cook really did her best.

Pat Lawrenson was given Horlicks to drink at school. And Shirley Landrum remembers, 'At seven (in 1941), I went to the Junior School, here they made us cocoa at playtime to keep us warm. Always hungry, I learned to eat lumpy spuds, grey gravy followed by thick rice pudding at dinnertime.' Shirley can remember in detail the available rations for the family:

From the age of four, I shopped with my grandma, we walked miles to the nearest Co-op shop, where they weighed everything and put it into blue paper bags… from the age of eight, I did the shopping for our rations. I knew exactly what I could have and carried it home. This was from a grocery store not far from home. On Saturdays I walked to the butcher in the next village. [This was Huyton, which is no longer considered to be a village.] Rations for four usually cost about five shillings (25 pence). At the back of each ration book was a given number of coupons called Points; these could be used for biscuits, tinned fruit or tinned fish. By the age of nine, I was an expert and Mum never minded what I chose. Maybe she did not like shopping.

It must have been difficult for mothers with young children to join these queues, when sometimes it took hours to reach the front. When Shirley was eight, her younger sister was only four. Perhaps Shirley's mother was glad to trust her capable older daughter to choose wisely for the family. Shirley continues:

Then I was allowed to join any queue… in the hope of getting oranges or bananas, both scarce. Sweets meant another queue, this time on Sunday morning, the only time the sweet shop opened. Mr Slater, a big, fat man kept us in order and his daughter, always called Miss Slater, served us one by one, carefully snipping out our precious sweet coupons. Not much choice, but we were glad of anything. Sometimes, during my Saturday shopping in Huyton, I would spend my pocket money on very strong mints or Horlicks tablets because they were not rationed. The chemist sold them. Didn't like either much at first, but grew to like them. Before he was a fireman, my Dad was a gardener, so grew our vegetables and soft fruit… gooseberries and raspberries… Granma made bread and used mashed potatoes in the mix to make it go further. We walked everywhere so we used up lots of energy, so fruit was made into puddings and pies. Meat had a crust added or dumplings, and few got fat.

Shirley also touches on the systems of barter, sale and exchange of goods and coupons. Some aspects of these deals were, strictly speaking, illegal, but the rules were complex and many people allowed common sense to rule their behaviour. Shirley says that her mother:

… had a friend who had eight children, who could not afford to buy all the sugar and sweets (to which her coupons entitled her), so Mum paid her for the extra coupons. Gave us the sweets and made jam with the fruit from the garden and the sugar.

Betty Harrison's aunt, on the farm in Howgill, 'had special baking days, bread, cakes etc. – everything made – butter, cheese, some of which she sold to the grocer who came every fortnight for his order by motorbike, It was a wonderful happy time.' Back at home, Betty remembers:

The variety of food was scarce. My father kept pigs, which, when one was slaughtered, we could barter. Also, when bananas came back, it was wonderful. I do not recall ever being short of food, as we grew so much ourselves.

Doreen Dalrymple remembers queuing, 'Saturday morning we spent in town (Southport) queuing for anything you could get... we never knew what we were queuing for – we just got in the queue and bought what was on offer.' This comment has been made by numerous people. If you found when you got to the front of the queue that the item was something you did not want, it could always be used as a 'swap' or given to another family member, who would reciprocate in due course.

Doreen's uncle also helped to provide food for the family, while her father was away in the Royal Engineers:

My uncle had been invalided out of the First World War and he got fish for us on the shore daily. Everyone shared in his catch. The pig farms used to get his eels... it was a good time of our lives, everyone helping each other... my uncle got some little ducks to fatten up for Christmas but no-one would eat them, so he gave them away. They had become pets to us.

But few people retained any sentimentality toward a potential source of food, even those who had not kept livestock before the war. For instance, Shirley Landrum remembers how her family's rations were supplemented, 'The rest of the meals were made of rabbit, which my Dad kept for meat (not cruel if you are hungry) and hens, which gave eggs and then meat.'
Bernard Browne recalls:

My sister, born in 1935, and I were very fortunate to have both our parents with us. My father no longer went to sea; he had a shore job involving shipping and my mother, who was a qualified shorthand typist was recruited to work for the national war effort. So, although a boy and only eleven when the war began, I did most of the shopping and spent many hours standing in queues, feeling quite out of my depth amongst the women who made up the best part of every queue. Often it was a question of 'first come, first served'. There was a good deal of exchanging goods with friends and neighbours; items of food they did not like or want, they took and swapped for something they needed. The odd rabbit was available and a sheep's head was a good asset for a nice pan of soup. Try and buy one today and they look at you as if you were from outer space!

There was a great deal of advice from the Ministry of Food intended to make rations go further. My mother's wartime recipe scrapbook contains numerous recipes for making rations go further and ways to add variety and interest to them. Some of the recipes have been crossed through, as if they had been tried but not enjoyed. Spam mould and turnip pie, along with stuffed cabbage, rabbit pudding and vegetable marrow chips, are amongst the recipes that have been cut out from other sources, such as women's magazines and newspaper articles.
Ministry of Food Fact Sheet No. 7, in a series entitled 'Making the most of', advised housewives to braise their Sunday joint. The possession of such an item may have seemed a little optimistic when the ration of meat per person per week was 1s to 2s.
People were sometimes tempted to obtain food by unorthodox methods. Maureen Sheehan, having been evacuated along with members of her extended family to Shawforth, near Rochdale, remembers a visit from her father, who was in the Fire Service in Liverpool:

The sheep used to come right down into the street daily. One time, my dad, who was a butcher pre-war, tried to get a lamb into our house by luring it with a piece of fat. The sheep smelt it and ran for its life!

SPAM MOULD

¼ lb. spam, ¼ lb. chopped cooked vegetables, 1 cooked beetroot, 1 tablespoon cooked haricot beans or cooked peas, ¼ oz. gelatine, 1 pint stock or water in which a meat cube has been dissolved, grated raw carrot, shredded raw cabbage

Melt the gelatine in a little of the hot stock or water, and add the rest of the liquid. Put in the chopped spam, cooked vegetables, beans or peas and half the beetroot cut into dice. Stir all together, pour into a wetted mould and leave to set. Serve in the centre of a platter with a border of grated carrot, shredded cabbage and sliced beetroot.

Serves 4 people.

'Spam Mould': this recipe is crossed through, which suggests it did not become a favourite!

Wartime rationing did not necessarily mean hardship or hunger. For many people in Liverpool, the 1930s had not been a time of comfort and plenty. Peter McGuiness comments:

> All dockers were employed as casual labour and, prior to the start of the war, my father was lucky to get two or three days work in a week. When a docker was not working there was no pay. Hence, conditions were hard for my father and mother. After the war began, many men were called up and there was a labour shortage… my father usually worked five and a half days a week and sometimes there was overtime. So during the war, we were better off than we were in peacetime.

Some of the aspects of rationing that were seen as great deprivation by middle-class housewives were viewed quite differently by the working-class woman trying to feed a family on rations. Offal, including liver, kidneys, tripe, hearts, trotters, heads and sweetbreads, was never rationed. Working-class women like Peter's mother, used to managing on a tight budget, were adept at producing tasty and extremely nourishing food for their families from this type of food. Middle-class women often disliked the appearance and the origins of offal and, even in the spirit of making the best of what was available, often struggled to learn how best to cook it in order to make dishes produced from offal acceptable to their families.

Joyce Morley had her tenth birthday in October 1939 and lived in Childwall. She actually suffered from malnutrition during the war years and did not really recover until 1952, when she was twenty-three years old. She recalls:

> What I most remember about the food situation during the war was that there was not a lot of it and certainly no variety. Before the war, in the 1930s, as my father was lucky enough to be in good and steady employment (unlike many, of course), my mother fed us a good staple diet. It came as a shock to experience feeling hungry for the first time.

Joyce goes on:

> My memory may deceive me, but I think we were reduced to about half a pound of sugar per week for a family of four. This might sound reasonable, but we were mostly a nation of

tea-drinkers then and the kettle was always on. Four of us, having at least one cup of tea per meal, with two teaspoonsful of sugar in each, soon whittled down the sugar ration. I had to cut down on sugar so much that I learnt to do without. To this day I don't use sugar on anything – cereals, grapefruits or strawberries. I cannot remember what the egg ration was, but it cannot have been very large as I mostly remember a substance called powdered egg, which was utterly tasteless. Because of the fat and egg limitations, cakes and biscuits were in very short supply. As the war continued, liquid paraffin was used to make cakes instead of butter or margarine. My mother used to visit a little family-owned cake shop in Allerton Road, called Palmer's Pastries. This small business carried on heroically all through the war, probably using liquid paraffin. They were quite tasty, considering we still talk of Palmer's P's, as we nicknamed them. My mother tried to give us plenty of stews. The meat ration was minimal and it wasn't long before the horrendous pseudo-meat known as 'spam' was shipped from America for us. It looked like a plastic mat; again, utterly tasteless. And you were supposed to dip it into the powdered egg mixture and fry it as spam fritters. Not much better was the tinned corned beef, also shipped from America; I believe, to stop us starving. I also remember the hideous cheese ration. It was largely darkish- red and looked like a block of soap.

Joan Gillett, from Walton, whose grandparents shared their large cellar air-raid shelter with neighbours, remembers the adults working together in other ways, 'Two maiden ladies next door used to pass some sweet coupons to us and some neighbours who kept hens in the back yard used to give us a few fresh eggs as a welcome change from the powdered variety.'

D. Hartley-Backhouse lived in Norris Green and attended the Liverpool Institute; he remembers putting his entrepreneurial skills to good use:

At school, at lunch-time, I went down to the cake shop in Berry Street, where I bought cakes for two pence and brought them back and sold them for three pence. Each week I cycled to my grandmother's bungalow in Llanfyllin, about 60-70 miles away. The egg ration was about one egg per week. But, being Welsh, the farmers sold me eggs and one day, I cycled from Llanfyllin home to Liverpool with five dozen eggs in my haversack, without breaking one.

The fresh eggs must have been welcomed by his friends and family.

Dried egg is recalled by many of the people who were children during the war years. Some people hated it whilst others enjoyed it as a supplement to their diet. It seems likely that the enjoyment of dried egg depended to a great extent on how one's mother learned to use it. For instance, some women used it to enable them to bake, thus keeping fresh eggs to be eaten. Pat Lawrenson's mother was one who managed to make dried egg enjoyable. Pat remembers it being used for omelettes and having it with sausages. Sausages were not rationed but were difficult to obtain. So Pat's mother had presumably queued for those that she remembers. Pat also says, 'We also had cheese on toast (which I didn't like) but you didn't have a choice – not like nowadays. Sometimes we had bread pudding (if you could get the dried fruit).' Both of these items suggest that Pat's mother was making a little go a long way. Cheese was rationed, but grated and placed sparsely on toast, it would go a lot further than cut in chunks on a sandwich. Bread pudding was filling and although bread was not rationed, it was not always readily available. However, Pat's father worked in a bakery, so perhaps there was some supply, in the form of staff sales, from this source. Some recipes for bread pudding actually recommend using stale bread, so this would be another way of making sure that nothing was wasted and yet offering the family palatable food. Bread pudding is very filling and the dried fruit, like the cheese, could be scattered sparingly throughout the mixture. Toast was made in front of the coal fire. Pat remembers, 'We had a toasting fork with a long handle. My dad made it.'

Jim McMurtry, born in 1942, was very young but still remembers how well his mother coped with rationing:

> My mother made the meat ration go a long way – casserole one day – stew the next – pastry on the left-overs on the third – always with fresh veg. But limited variety – cabbage or carrots and turnips, usually. There were very few fresh eggs so powdered eggs were used regularly. When the first fresh eggs were readily available after the war, I remember painting boiled eggs many colours for Easter.

Elva Barooah remembers:

> We did quite well as regards food. My mother was industrious and ingenious at getting it. I know there were long queues; every Saturday lunch time, we queued at the fish and chip shop; we had to take a bowl as there was no wrapping paper. A neighbour had relatives in the country who had hens; whenever she went there, she sold us fresh eggs and my mother was friendly with the pressed meat pork shop owner and used to get meat from her, secretly, without coupons. We had spam and, I think, corned beef. We had a cooked breakfast with dried, scrambled eggs. At some later stage, my mother made me scrambled egg with a real egg. She was amused when I said that I preferred the 'real' scrambled egg made with dried egg. On Saturdays, we had pig's trotters, crab or other shell fish. I remember the appearance of ration books but was only really affected by the sweet coupons. Again, we never felt any shortage; we had my parents' sweet ration. We used to get 2 oz (two ounces) of sweets to go to the pictures. My mother said that she didn't like sweets.

TURNIP PIE

4 medium sized turnips, 3 tablespoons milk, 2 tablespoons fat, 3 tablespoons dried breadcrumbs, 3 tablespoons grated cheese, seasoning

Cook the diced turnips in boiling salt water for about fifteen minutes. Drain, saving about five tablespoons of the liquid to add to the milk. Melt the fat and mix with the breadcrumbs and cheese. Put a layer of turnips into a greased baking dish, then spread over with a thin layer of cheese mixture. Add another layer of turnip and another of cheese mixture, using up these ingredients. Season to taste. Pour over the milk and liquor, and bake for twenty minutes, or until the turnips are quite tender and the top breadcrumbs are brown.

Cooking time: about 40 minutes.   Serves 4 people.

Turnip Pie must have been more successful!

It seems more than likely that Elva's mother preferred to see her daughters enjoying her sweet ration to eating the sweets herself. Elva continues:

> Once my sister was holding the coupons and a gust of wind whirled them onto the railway track at Orrell Park Station. Catastrophe! My father went into the station and walked along the track to retrieve them – I thought it was dangerous! We bought packets of ice-cream wafers to eat. Some horrible sweets – Victory V lozenges and sulphur sweets and some very strong liquorice sticks were off-ration. We ate them doggedly. My sister made some sweets with cocoa and rolled them in dried milk powder. I remember seeing disused chocolate machines and wondering what it would be like to get chocolate out of a machine. There was Camp coffee – like treacle – disgusting! To drink, we had tea, usually. Lemonade, sometimes, or Dandelion and Burdock. Tizer for treats!

Margaret Barber's memories are shared with her brother, Ernest, a year younger than Margaret, and sister, Sheila, only five when the war began. Their mother became ill after giving birth to their youngest sister, Elizabeth, and died in July 1940. Their father was in the RAF, so after a period of being cared for by their grandmother, the children went to live with their aunt and uncle. Margaret pays tribute to her aunt, 'Although being fifty-three, my Aunt Margaret took us to her home. There were five of us, six with the baby and we were brought up very well.'

Margaret Barber remembers some of the meals that she and her family enjoyed during the war. She remarks:

> We were lucky as the rations worked out well with a family of eight. My aunt was a good manager and cook; we had dripping and toast, lobscouse made with the bone from the week-end joint; hotpot; bacon on top of potato and onion in a deep dish; corned beef (part of the meat ration) made into a pie with potato and onion, carrots and celery; Cheese Dreams (which were cheese sandwiches fried) absolutely delicious!; stuffed marrow and marrow and ginger jam. As my uncle had an allotment, we were never short of lovely vegetables. He also kept bantams in his garden for the eggs. We were able to buy fish and herrings were very cheap. 9d a pound, I remember. For a party, we couldn't get any biscuits for the younger children, so we spread lemon cheese on ice-cream wafers and sandwiched them together. They went down a treat!

In 1943, Margaret was fifteen and went as an assistant teacher at a Preparatory School, 'The head did all the cooking for dinner. She made big milk puddings with barley flakes and macaroni instead of rice. Always a jam tart too.'

Margaret also points out that Southport was not so safe as had been thought:

> Bombers let go of stray bombs on their return journey from bombing Liverpool docks. One night, my uncle, Jack Sawyer, was fire-watching when a land-mine hit the Sunshine Home for Blind Babies. We couldn't understand why he was so quiet when he came home next day. Later, our aunt told us that he was haunted by all those young lives lost.

On another occasion:

> Our school was hit by a land-mine one night. We were in a shelter on the corner of Grantham Road; it was a heavy raid and several houses were hit in Birkdale and Southport. The lady from the 'chippy' sent her husband to count us all when the shop closed and kept cooking until we all got a bag of chips. She also made cocoa for the young children.

Enid Johnston remembers another generous action and captures the extra depth of enjoyment of a treat that is rare as well as unexpected, 'I remember sometimes having to have lessons in private houses and, one memorable day, the lady whose house we were in produced a chocolate finger each. Such a small thing, but, to us, sheer heaven.'

People attempted to make light of the shortages; a cartoon character named Mr Chad was created, who appeared to peer over a fence. The captions which accompanied him always highlighted an article that was in particularly short supply at that time – 'WOT! No bananas?' 'WOT! No stockings?' For children, the ever-present scarcity was 'WOT! No sweets?'

Temptation proved too much on one occasion for normally well-behaved Evelyn and Audrey, who were evacuated to stay in a sweet shop in Ormskirk:

> My friend and I were particularly naughty one night. We got up out of bed in the dark and, with no-one about, crept downstairs and through the door at the bottom into the shop. The lure of the sweet shop was too tempting for us! We quickly confiscated a packet of Maltesers. Back in bed, we ate one or two and suddenly felt frightened at what we had done. One of us came up with the bright idea of getting rid of the incriminating evidence by throwing the rest of them out of our bedroom window. This we did, only to hear them clatter like the sound of large hailstones as they hit the corrugated tin roof of the shed below. We were mortified! But we never did anything like that again, and no-one ever mentioned it.

Arthur Williams also remembers occasional treats:

> Now and then, one of the boy's fathers came home from abroad with bananas and oranges which were not available in the shops… the school would then raffle them for 1*d* a time. The money went to help to buy ammunition for the war. We didn't have sweets but we had what looked like a wood substance called sticky lice [liquorice root] and it tasted of liquorice. The bread we had was black bread; we also had dried egg, dried milk – but we were allowed one fresh egg per person per month.

Evelyn Davies was evacuated to a sweet shop in Ormskirk with her friend, Audrey Jump.

This should have been one fresh egg per person per week, but the egg supply was unreliable. Many people began to keep their own hens, even in back yards. Arthur continues:

> A main meal would consist of potatoes, carrots and gravy but no meat. Our next door neighbour used to kill his pigeons and sometimes gave us a couple. We used to buy food from the allotments, such as rhubarb and vegetables. People also grew what they could at home even if they only had a back yard. When meat was available, word got around. People would rush to queue but, maybe, by the time they got to be served the meat would be sold out. Some of the food we did eat when available was mince, pig's head, sheep's head, pig's feet and brawn.

Alan Bentley, who lived in Gilman Street, off Walton Breck Road, was only three when the war began and had the belief in magic of a young child, 'I remember that we used to play in Stanley Park and, at the Wishing Well, I asked for a Mars bar and a banana, which were unobtainable during wartime.'

Gordon Crompton and his friends had more practical ways of enlivening their wartime rations. The 'cast-iron shore', or 'Cassy' as it was known, was near to Gordon's home in Aigburth. It was so-called because, in the Victorian period, the iron ore came in and was landed there from barges supplying the Liverpool foundries. During this era the foundries produced cast iron of high quality and in huge quantities. The name survived in local usage. Gordon recalls that:

> … a ship was sunk by enemy action near the bar at the entrance to the River Mersey, and amongst its other cargo, it was carrying enough oranges to feed an army. Those oranges being washed ashore on the Cassy were dumped on a field close by. To get to the oranges, you had to climb a high wall which was beyond most kids, except Muggins and several other lads (girls weren't up to such antics in those days). We always made sure when pinching oranges that they had not been pierced in any way before eating them. One day, I was rummaging in one of the orange mountains when I had a feeling I was being watched. I looked up and there, no more than a couple of yards away, sat a rat as big as a small cat. I didn't bother to hang around and never returned to the place again! You must remember that most fruit, with the exception of, maybe, apples and pears, were gold dust in those dark days, especially oranges and bananas.

Families would welcome food from various sources, especially if it offered a change. Monica Hoban, who lived in Woodbine Street, Kirkdale, remembers that her mother managed well:

> Food was rationed, but we managed to eat quite well. I think we had a lot of home-made chips. We had a lot of rabbit and plenty of veg. My father kept chickens in the back yard, so we had some eggs, and now and then a chicken, but we couldn't eat it. They all had names, so we didn't feel like eating Lizzie or one of the others. Sausages were made mostly of bread. We had spam, dried egg, and we had home-made cake – eggless sponge – how housewives managed to organise meals I'll never know.

There were occasional treats:

> My Dad worked on the docks and sometimes an American ship would dock and the sailors gave bars of chocolate and comics away; plus my cousin, who lived with us, was in the Navy on the Russian convoys. He used to bring some food home; mostly tea, we never had coffee. He also brought a loaf of bread. It was white. The bread we were able to buy was grey, almost black. It tasted awful, but we ate it.

Monica's cousin must have been aware that a plain loaf of white bread was now a welcome luxury. The coarse, greyish National Loaf was what was available. It was made with more of the grain than was used for white bread, and was not universally popular, although some people liked it toasted. Bread was never sliced or wrapped during the war years as an economy measure and this restriction remained in place until 1950.

Marjorie Greenwood, living in Havelock Street, remembers a kind baker, 'I remember people queuing for bread, mostly it was brown, but Mr Watts, the baker, sometimes used to treat us and let us have a white loaf.'

Frances Jennings was ten years old in 1939. She remembers that:

> … as Christmas 1940 approached food became more scarce; the un-rationed goods were harder to find but 'bush telegraph' was used and a queue would form outside food shops and it was not unusual to wait up to an hour to be served, if there was anything left. Fish and chip shops opened for about two hours but the queue was so long that the chips and fish would be finished before you got near to be served. A lot of people turned their garden over to growing potatoes and vegetables and, providing they could get the fat, they made their own chips. Fish shops opened for two hours on two or three days a week and some unheard-of fish was on sale.

Fish was never actually rationed, but Britain's fishing grounds were vulnerable to U-boats. One of the unheard-of varieties to which Frances refers was whale-meat. It was described as tasting like cod-liver oil, which seems logical, and also like a fishy sort of liver. Frances goes on:

Potatoes were filling and nutritious – a Ministry of Food poster.

Ice-cream shops had already disappeared (by 1940), especially the Italian ones; the dairies only sold milk, there was no cream. But it was possible to buy dried apricots, dried apple which helped. Other dried goods were eggs, mashed potato and dried milk to make custard.

Reg Cox, evacuated in 1940 to North Wales, remembers that:

At Greenfield, we were 'in the country' and things like rabbits were available, and spuds etc. grew in the garden, so we ate well, but I was an eleven-year-old lad, and you can never fill one of those.

The impact of rationing in the countryside was often less severe because of swapping and bartering. People tended to have more land and to be used to growing vegetables. They were therefore better at it. People living in cottages, not just on farms, kept hens, bees, even pigs. Many evacuees benefited from this traditional lifestyle, although this was not always true.

Jim Williams was evacuated from Toxteth to Four Mile Bridge, near Holyhead. 'Well, it was not the happiest of times. We had more dinner hours than dinners.' However, rescue was at hand. Jim's father was at sea and his ship called in at Holyhead:

He came to see us and took us home; some kids had a good time away, but not us. Anyway, it was back to the greatest city in the world! We got back for the worst winter in years, but that did not worry us. We were home.

By 1944, Reg Cox was fifteen and back home:

As the war progressed, rationing became tighter and tighter. How my mother kept me fed I don't know, but I can remember being very hungry. My mother used to send me down to a baker's shop, near to Wavertree Town Hall, in the hope of buying bread, which was not only rationed, but in very short supply.

In fact, bread was not actually rationed during the war years, but shortages made it seem as if this was the case. Reg continues:

Our main groceries were purchased in Carson's at the junction of Penny Lane and Smithdown Road. A classic old grocer's shop, where, if you bought some sugar, they'd take a piece of flat blue paper and fold it into a bag that stayed in place without any adhesive or tape. Butter was cut from a block and banged into shape with two pieces of wood before being wrapped.

During the war years, of course, both sugar and butter were rationed and customers would also be expected to keep wrapping papers for re-use as paper was also in short supply. Reg's sister, Pat, was stationed in Hereford:

… married to a lovely Welshman she'd met in the R.A.F. Stan could charm the birds off the trees and would send us food parcels, black market butter and cheese that he managed to organise. We used to look forward to these gifts from heaven, but one day we received a parcel from Stan and, when we opened it, instead of butter and cheese, it contained several blocks of 'Monkey Brand', an abrasive block for cleaning doorsteps. Someone had intercepted our much longed-for delights, we never did find out who… well, we could hardly go to the Police, could we?

Chapter Ten

Mothers, Fathers and Other Adults

In wartime, children met adults who would never have been part of their lives in ordinary circumstances. Sometimes this was through evacuation or because service people were billeted in their homes or in their towns. Children saw people of many different nationalities, such as Free French, Poles and US servicemen.

The arrival of US troops in Liverpool after 1942 is remembered by a number of the children. Many Americans arrived in this country through Liverpool, and there were some camps in the area. Frederick Berwick says, 'We were fascinated by them. They looked so smart in their uniforms and leather jackets. We would always ask "Got any gum, chum?"'

Jim McMurtry also recalls:

> I remember American soldiers visiting a certain house in our street and sitting on the window sills. We were too young to understand what was going on! But we appreciated the Juicy Fruits and chewing gum doled out to us!

America enters the war. *Good Housekeeping*, November 1942, shows the Stars and Stripes with the Union Jack.

It was not just children who saw the US troops as a source of many items that were scarce in ration-weary Britain. Elva Barooah remembers that:

> Our neighbourhood in Walton was ultra-respectable. I don't remember seeing men in American uniform, but I knew that Burtonwood meant something bad, and, just once, when we were at a tram stop, there were some girls somehow fooling about with young men. My mother said something disparaging about girls and Americans which drew my attention to them.

Burtonwood was a supply and maintenance base for the US Air Force in Europe. It was near Warrington and some girls from the surrounding areas, including Liverpool, would go out there to dances. This was widely disapproved. Burtonwood was responsible for thirty other bases in the UK and about 70,000 personnel. It provided new bombers and fighters for US squadrons and was also responsible for their upkeep. It was nicknamed 'Lancashire's Detroit' by the Americans. There were also smaller US camps in Lancashire, such as the three in Maghull. The problem with young women coming in search of nylons, chocolate and a good time was dealt with at Maghull Station by local police officers waiting for the Liverpool trains and leading the girls over the footbridge onto the other platform and seeing them onto the Liverpool-bound trains for their return journey.

The Americans were also remembered by Gordon Crompton, 'We had the Yanks camped on the perimeter track in Sefton Park and we kids used to cadge candy and chocolate off them, until they got fed up with us and chased us off!' Gordon also remembers some British airmen, one of whom gave Gordon an exciting moment:

> The next door neighbours, namely the Hudsons, had a son, Leslie, who was a pilot and they told us that he would be flying over our houses that afternoon. Sure enough the aircraft came over our houses flying very low – I think it was a Hurricane.

Gordon continues:

> During those dark days, we had three airmen billeted with us and two of them actually slept with me in the same bed in the attic. We had a four-bedroom house in Allington Street, Aigburth. I vividly remember one of the airmen had smelly feet and the other snored incessantly; otherwise, it was great, as sleeping with grown men made me feel ten feet tall. Unfortunately, one of these men was posted to Africa and I heard later that he had been killed in action. This made me feel very sad as he was a very nice man.

Children had experiences that made them grow up quickly and, also, made them realise that the adults in their lives were vulnerable in a way that would not have dawned upon them until they were much older in peacetime.

Elizabeth Charles was born in 1933, and she tells of the tragic loss of her father and baby brother:

> In the May Blitz, a landmine fell on the front step of my parents' house. My father was an ARP warden at the time and he had returned to see if my mother and baby brother (nine months old) were OK. My father and baby brother were killed and my mother seriously injured. I was not told at the time and, in fact, did not know until I had returned home [from evacuation to Westbury, near Shrewsbury] in 1944. I feel it has made a great impact on my life and I would not like to go through all that again.

The resilience and stoicism contained in this understatement is typical of many of the children who suffered loss of parents and siblings, but wanted to be brave and patriotic. Many of them are telling their stories for the first time now, and still show a remarkable disinclination to complain. This attitude must be quite astonishingly brave to today's generation, used as they are to the offer of 'counselling' for many comparatively minor setbacks in life.

Evelyn Davies returned to her home at the Fire Station in Bootle from evacuation in Ormskirk when there was a lull in the bombing attacks; she remembers the courage of the adults in the Fire Station community in the presence of the children, and the undaunted spirit of the firemen who fought to save their city from the flames that threatened to engulf it.

> After some weeks (the raids) started again but much worse than ever. Luckily we had our own underground air raid shelter at the Fire Station. Quite often it was about 6pm at night when the noise of the siren would start. On hearing it, mothers and children would make their way down the flights of stone steps. It was like an exodus.
>
> Each family would be ready with blankets, cushions, a hot drink in a thermos flask, maybe a book or two or some knitting. If the siren went later in the evening, mothers and children would be in their nightwear with a warm coat on top. We could hear the almost monotonous drone of the German planes flying overhead and got used to their particular sound. I think people held their breath, praying they would go away. You could also hear and feel the blast of a bomb exploding in the surrounding areas and the dockside. News would filter down to the shelter that fires could be seen glowing in the distance. We knew Liverpool had been hit badly. If our parents were frightened, they managed not to show it for our sakes. The firemen would return from their duties with blackened faces from the smoke and fires they had dealt with, all looking weary but with no time to sleep.

Firemen at the Fire Salvage Depot, Derby Street, Bootle, with local dignitaries, just before the war. Most of the older officers have First World War medals, including Evelyn Davies' father (second from right, middle row).

Sadly, the gallant Fire Service community were not to escape the ever-present dangers of the Blitz.

> My Uncle Dave was a Fire Salvage Officer at Hatton Garden Fire Salvage Station, which was in the centre of Liverpool, and he and his family lived 'on the premises', as we did. One night of heavy bombing, he left his wife and two girls of twelve and fourteen in the station air raid shelter, while he went home to make them a flask of tea. In that short time a bomb hit the part of the shelter where they were, and they were killed. My mother and father were heartbroken to lose his dear sister, Doris, and nieces, Joan and Rene, but he carried on his job just the same.

Olive Woods lost two uncles, one a captain in the Merchant Navy, and the other a Chief Petty Officer in the Royal Navy. The latter 'was in HMS *Kelly* that went down at the Battle of Crete. Earl Mountbatten was the Captain and he was saved along with some others, but my uncle was not one of them.' She was immortalised as HMS *Torrin* in the 1942 film *In Which We Serve*, starring Noel Coward as Earl Mountbatten, and John Mills as one of the crew.

David Buckley had an older cousin:

> He was a pilot and came to visit us when he was on leave. After he had been with us for a few hours, he had to go back and was going to get his train at Lime Street station. He asked if my sister and I would like to go with him to town to catch his train, which we did. When we got down there, we found that his train was delayed and there were a couple of hours to spare, so he asked us if we would like to go to the Tatler theatre for a while. It was a News and Cartoon cinema on Church Street. After we saw him off, that was the last time we ever saw him, as a couple of weeks later, he was shot down and killed.

Lawrence Whittaker's father, Joe Whittaker, served aboard the SS *Oropesa* in the Merchant Navy. He was lost at sea, when the *Oropesa* was torpedoed in the Atlantic on 16 January 1941. Lawrence remembers:

> When my mother went to collect his pay after she had received the telegram to tell her that he had been killed, there was so little money to come that she had to walk home from Liverpool because she hadn't enough money for the tram fare. If your ship was lost before midday, you were only due half a day's pay for the day you were lost. Later my mother, Hilda, went to work on the Royal Ordnance Factory to earn enough to keep us. Many years later, my mother and I met and shook hands with the Queen and Prince Philip when she unveiled the Memorial on Tower Hill.

On 5 November 1955, Queen Elizabeth II unveiled the Tower Hill Memorial to the Merchant Navy and Fishing Fleets, with the names from 1939-1945 in addition to those of the First World War already inscribed. Thirty-year-old Able Seaman Joe Whittaker's name is on the memorial, along with many others lost at sea.

Even when the adults in their family were not killed, there were other aspects of war to be faced, which were, at best, unpleasant, and at worst deeply traumatic, both physically and emotionally.

Children were realising that while most adults were caring and did their best for them in these dangerous times, others were unkind and caused children to have some less happy experiences to recount. These contrasts were thrown into sharp relief by differing experiences of evacuation.

Donald Hunter, aged four, was evacuated with his sister, Hilda, aged six, and brother, George, aged nine, to Bleddfa, near Knighton, Radnorshire, in 1939. They were all pupils at Bedford Road School in Bootle. George was billeted on a hill-farm, 'a very nice place, where he assisted with farm work and learned to ride.' But Donald and Hilda had instructions not to be separated. Donald recalls:

> We were the last two to be housed with a Mrs Watson, who accepted us under duress. We were not happy. Any food my brother brought down to us, we did not get it. Her little girl, about my age, had more than her share. Mrs Watson didn't starve us but didn't feed us well. Her daughter would always receive second helpings but we wouldn't be offered any. Although Mrs Watson did not make me work, she did make my sister do extra chores. Once, when my mother and father came down to see us, and stayed with us until they had to leave for their train, my sister told me not to cry, so it wouldn't upset them, but, at that tender age, I lost control and sobbed. My parents suspected that we were not happy at all. My mother related her uneasiness to the authorities and Bootle Education sent Mr Ralston from the School Board to Bleddfa. When he arrived, my sister was cleaning the step and she was ill. Later it was found that she had scabies and I had mumps. Mr Ralston removed us from the house and had us sent to the Vicarage. We stayed there for the rest of the time we were evacuated and we were very happy, with plenty of room to roam and play.

Mr Ralston emerges from this story as the hero, who restored Donald's faith in human nature. Donald says, 'Later Mr Ralston was one of my school masters at Balliol Road School. He was a gentleman.' He told Donald later that Mrs Watson was taken to court in respect of her treatment of Donald and his brave big sister, Hilda, who, like many children, had wanted to spare their parents any anxiety. Donald and his sister went back to Wales on a number of occasions to see Elsie Williams, the daughter of the Vicarage caretaker, as she had helped to care for them in their time at the Vicarage.

Also in Wales, a little girl remembers the couple with whom her sister was staying. Beryl Redfern was seven when the war began and she and her sister were evacuated after their house was damaged in May 1941. She remembers:

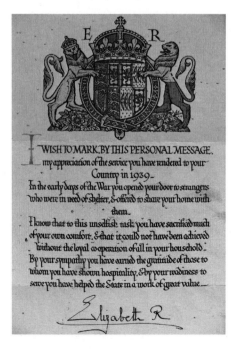

Queen Elizabeth sent a personal message of appreciation to evacuee host families. This certificate was sent to Mrs Edwards who had welcomed Vic Smith to Bagillt, North Wales. Vic kept in touch with the family until 1999.

Miss Edith Mather was a wonderful
hostess in Birkdale to four Bootle
Grammar School Girls.

When we got to Wales, we all stood in a row and people came along to choose us. When it
came to our turn, my sister and I were split up because nobody would take two children.
I lived in a small cottage and had to wash my hair in a big tub which stood outside in the cold.
My sister, Elsie, three years younger than me, lived in a big house on a hill and I would have
to walk a long way to call for her to go to school. She was staying with Mr and Mrs Pinnigar,
who were caretakers of the Chapel. I would spend a lot of time there polishing the pews –
I would have tea with them and start the long walk home. I do not know how long we were
evacuated.

Irene Stephenson had a very happy experience of evacuation from Bootle to Birkdale,
near Southport. She has vivid memories of her hostess, a middle-aged spinster, and of her
welcome to Irene and her schoolfriends:

Miss Mather looked at us and we looked at her 'Come inside, you must be ready for something to eat!' Somehow, four thirteen-year-old schoolgirls and one middle-aged spinster
gelled on sight. Right away we felt at home. It was to be a happy time in our lives, an experience that helped us stand on our own feet, although she invited our parents to visit us at
weekends. Some girls went home because they were unhappy in their billets. The girls with
Miss Mather had no such problems. In school each week a register was called and each girl
asked if she was alright in her billet. On reaching our four names, Miss Graham, our form mistress, would say 'Oh, you're with Miss Mather!' That meant all was well. Miss Edith Mather was
then about forty-five years old, the same age as my mother. She and my mother became firm
friends, and, after we girls went home, they kept in touch and visited each other. Through that
contact, I learned a little of Miss Mather's life. As a young woman, her fiancé was killed in France,

so when the First World War ended, she had to find work. She became housekeeper to a family in Cheshire, living in a large house, where she stayed for many years. She learned a lot about looking after people and eventually, she saved enough to buy the house in Birkdale and began to take weekly guests for holidays. Many of them returned every year. She had built up a good little business, but then came the Second World War and she was landed with four evacuees. The Government paid the princely sum of eight shillings and sixpence per child per week to people who took evacuees. It was not a large amount, but she kept four big girls well-fed.

Miss Mather died in the late nineteen-fifties. She had given her evacuees, very unobtrusively, a great deal of tender, loving care. After the war, when we heard about the dreadful things that had happened to some evacuees, we realised just how lucky we had been. Even today, when any of the girls get together, there is generally some little memory of Miss Mather.

Ray Brundrit was ten in 1939 and lived in Hartwood Road, Southport. This did not spare his family from the full force of war. He recounts:

My Dad was an electrical contractor and directed to war work, an arms factory (Brockhouse) on the outskirts of town... it was camouflaged but it was hit, more by chance, and with only one fatality. Dad was very shaken up – he didn't seem the same person and passed away shortly after in 1941, aged 36. In those days, there were no pensions, so Mum had to take work of any kind, and, although she was not in good health herself, she went to war work in the same factory.

Ray left school at fourteen on a Friday and started work on the next Monday. He enjoyed 'getting a good wage packet' and remembers that 'Mum shouted "We're rich"' when he handed it over. This sort of solidarity with lone mothers and a sympathetic understanding of their problems, whether widows or with husbands who were away, comes through very strongly. Most children grew up quickly. It was often impossible to shield them from difficulties and mothers often needed older children to share their problems or needed to explain shortages to younger children by simply telling them the true situation.

In spite of the circumstances, mothers and fathers tried their best to give children as normal a childhood as possible. But even when there was no bereavement, loss of home or other disaster, this was difficult in wartime. Families, friends and even acquaintances made great adjustments in order to help each other.

Patricia Blamire remembers:

At a late stage in the war, my mother opened the door to find a family who had been bombed out, looking for shelter. They were people who had bought a shop in Liscard from my father's cousin, several years previously. Their daughter, Bernice, had been machine-gunned in the back-yard and was severely traumatised. There were five of them, the parents, Bernice, an aunt and a cousin, but, somehow, my parents managed to find room for them. They managed to re-open the shop, so went there every day, returning to us at night. Life was very cramped, but we managed for a number of months. Unfortunately, their huge Old English sheepdog had to remain at the shop as we just couldn't squeeze him in!

Joan and Jim McMurtry's mother was a capable person who had managed to create stability for her children while her husband was at sea. But Joan remembers:

Two of our aunties and their families were 'bombed out'. They all came to us. In a small terraced house, this must have presented problems but Mum was the kind who coped. My more histrionic Aunt Isabelle used to have hysterics whenever she heard the sirens and run round the kitchen in circles.

Jim says:

> Looking back I am amazed how most people coped and showed great character. People constantly dropped in for cups of tea, through ever-open doors. Throughout the war, our mother remained strong – standing in queues for whatever was going – knitting all hours – keeping us amused and remaining positive and cheerful – a great example.

Surely this tribute from her son would be ample reward!

Pam Fawcett and her sister, Gillian Skinner, née Mylchreest, lived in Heliers Road, Clubmoor. Gillian was born in 1940, and Pam herself was only three years old when the war began:

> I am sure other people have more interesting tales to tell you, but I do remember sitting under the stairs with my special doll, behind the pram in which my sister was asleep, and hearing the Air Raid Warden shouting to put the light out, which was only a candle. Another thing was watching my grandmother open packets of tea and sugar, making sure every grain was carefully removed from all the corners of the wrapping paper.

This is a memory that was character forming for a whole generation; many people who were children during the war years have commented that they have remained careful all their lives and are horrified by waste; making sure sugar bags are empty; scraping butter and margarine wrappers, or, in recent years, tubs; saving buttons from old clothes and using soap and toothpaste to the last minute amount.

Pam also pays tribute to their mother:

> I feel I had a very secure childhood; my mother always made us happy and comfortable. One of our greatest delights was having our mother's brother come home on leave from the Merchant Navy; he always had gifts for us, toys, sweets and fruit he had purchased at the places he docked. He was in the Atlantic Convoys.

This is one example of how some children were fortunate enough to be protected from the grim realities of wartime, since serving in the Atlantic Convoys was extremely perilous. Yet at the time, these two little girls, Pam and Gillian, were shielded from adult anxiety about their uncle. This must have been part of their mother's determination that the war should not impinge too much on their childhood. This meant that other adult activities connected with the war did not seem threatening. Pam remembers 'We had a Barrage Balloon Station in the grounds of the school at the top of our road, watching the man climb our garden walls to retrieve it, if ever a balloon came down, always proved exciting.'

Enid Johnston's mother also did her best for the family. Enid says:

> My mother, as all mothers were, was very good at making things to tempt us to eat. One speciality was sweets made from National Dried milk, and usually a lurid green from the cake colourings of the time – if anyone had any left. One thing we had to eat, though I never managed it, was brawn, and I can still remember how awful it was and how we hated it. Mother would join endless queues to see if she could get a cake for us to make up for the brawn.

Enid's mother died in 1943. There is some evidence that women were especially vulnerable to infection and illness during the war years. This was perhaps because of the anxiety about their families, and partly, perhaps, because they were giving the larger share of the rations to the rest of the family and lacked the nourishment that they needed for good health.

Doris Scott, née Chambers, lived in Hawkins Street and was nine when the war began. She says, 'When I was twelve, my mother died from pneumonia through neglecting herself.' Doris then went to live with her father and half-sister in Everton. After being taught 'in a house up the street on certain half-days of the week – I never really caught up with my maths'. Doris also changed school and went to Skerry's College; she remembers, 'the smell of doughnuts frying as we walked up Mount Pleasant.' Doughnuts were being offered for sale in Liverpool because of the arrival of the Americans and Australians, 'looking very glamorous, just like the cinema!'

Some children found that although people did not always behave in the same way as their own family, they did have kind hearts. Joan Tisdale was a member of a happy family separated by war:

> My beloved mother died and most of my family were in the Forces; my Dad had to do ARP duty, so, with no-one to look after me, I was evacuated to Wales. It was not a happy time, but, I must stress, the family I was billeted with did not treat me unkindly, but they didn't show any warmth or friendliness, and, having come from a warm, loving family, it was so lonely. After the May Blitz, I learnt that my Dad was in hospital with injuries from shrapnel. My landlady invited my dad to come and recuperate with us when he came out of hospital, which he did. He looked so old and grey, I hardly recognised him. My Dad was excused any further ARP duty, so I was allowed to go home to be with him. I was so happy to be back home.

Joan Gillett, who had waved her father off to war in 1942, remembers his return in 1946. She was eight years old:

Children kept in touch by letter with distant family members. *Good Housekeeping*, Christmas Issue, 1943.

My Dad served in Burma – he came home in July 1946. He was delayed because he was ill with malaria. He walked from Lime Street station in the early hours of the morning and threw stones at the front bedroom window in order to wake my Mum to let him in. Next morning I came downstairs to find my dad asleep on the couch. He had yellow skin after suffering from malaria and seemed very thin. On his first evening home, my Dad took me to Stanley Park to a visiting funfair. I felt uneasy in his company as though he was a stranger and it took some time to get to know him again. It took my sister, only four years old, even longer to get to know him, but eventually it all turned out as it should and we both became very close to him. Mum told us he suffered from nightmares and used to jump up from sleep and try to get into the wardrobe away from the Japs. He did not like my sister and me to make too much noise as his nerves were shattered. He also suffered from bouts of malaria and the doctor was a frequent visitor to our house. There was no such thing as counselling. People got over their traumas in the healing of time. The war certainly affected our lives and must have left some scars to this day. However, we got our beloved father back from hell and he lived to seventy-seven years of age. We count ourselves lucky to have had those years with him as so many others did not have that pleasure.

Dorothy Pemberton, née Bartlett, was eleven when the war began and lived in Aspen Grove with her parents and two small brothers. She remembers her father:

My father had been unemployed but was now working with the Rescue Party, ARP, helping people from bombed property. There were times when we didn't know where he was – night after night – no phones for us then! We spent most of our nights in a shelter in our small backyard. Very cosy but crowded. My father made three bunk beds for us. We had a wicker lamp – egg-shaped with paraffin oil inside, with a little dial to wind the wick up and down. My father also built a door on the shelter and attached a sheet of tarpaulin with holes to ventilate it. He also built a little shelf to put an alarm clock, torch, keys, insurance policies, valuables, ration books on – just in case the house went on fire. He thought of everything!

Olive Woods remembers her father keeping a cool head when a landmine was dropped in Thornton Street, Litherland, where they lived, 'Many of us were hurt; one lady had lost her leg and my father, who had only just passed his First Aid, attended her until an ambulance came. He did a wonderful job.'

Most people were determined to 'carry on', to 'do their bit', to keep their nerve and not let each other down. David Buckley's father had already served his country in the First World War and lost a leg, so as he was unable to volunteer as an Air Raid Warden. David remembers that 'my Mum went in his place and had to go and learn how to put out an incendiary bomb fire with a stirrup pump, which was supplied to her and kept in the house.'

Albert Lewis recalls:

People always congregated in the street after an air raid when the ARP wardens (who had telephone contact with their colleagues) would indicate which other local areas had been damaged. Looking back on those days, one can only admire the behaviour of the adults who must have understood the desperate circumstances that were present when, perhaps, their children did not fully appreciate what was taking place, but they were always protective and there was never a hint of fear or panic. All the local people contributed to a friendly, organized and sympathetic aspect of the dreadful events occurring before our very eyes!

Chapter Eleven

The Lighter Side of the War!

'For entertainment, we had the radio on endlessly' remembers Elva Barooah. 'I remember *ITMA* and what it stood for, but I didn't understand it'

The programme *ITMA* was broadcast as a trial in July 1939, and returned as a series in September 1939; it was extremely popular. *ITMA* stood for 'It's That Man Again!' and was a popular catchphrase at the time. 'That man' was Hitler and every time he made some territorial claim or encroachment, the newspapers headlines would read 'It's That Man Again!' *ITMA* was Tommy Handley's show, and like a number of other popular wartime comedians, he was from Liverpool. Tommy was born in Aigburth and the characters from his show were said to be based on his observations of Liverpool people, but they struck a chord with the whole nation. The catchphrases were on everyone's lips, including those of children. Handley's exclamation 'Well, I'll go to the foot of our stairs!' was as well-known as those remembered by Elva, such as the catchphrases of Mrs Mopp and Mona Lott.

Elva continues:

'Can I do you now, sir?' (Mrs Mopp) and 'It's being so cheerful that keeps me going!' (Mona Lott) were catch-phrases that everyone knew. We were taken to the cinema often – maybe two or three times a week – often to see adult films. I think baby-sitters were unheard-of and my parents were film fans. I didn't mind and knew all the big names of the era – James Mason, Margaret Lockwood etc. At the end, we rushed out to avoid the National Anthem, but, if it started, we were stuck and had to stand to attention with everyone else. We went to 'First House', which ended quite early and came home in the dark with a torch. Saturday afternoons I always went with my sister and friends to the Children's Saturday Matinee – Tarzan or cowboys.

The torch used by Elva's parents must have been the permitted small pocket torch. However, the appropriate batteries were not always easily obtained and a larger torch could not be used instead. Elva says, 'I remember wardens shouting "Put that light out" if any house showed a light, but had no thoughts about the reason. From time to time local houses and a church were bombed. I just accepted it as normal.'

The radio played a very important role for adults in wartime in informing and educating, although the news programmes could also be worrying for children who were away from home. Joan Tisdale, evacuated to Wales, remembers, 'We just knew from the radio that Liverpool was being badly bombed'. However, the radio was mainly a morale booster and the only real entertainment. This was especially true for children who had been used to visits to the local cinema; now the nearest cinema was often many miles from some of the safe areas in the deep countryside.

For one boy, thirteen-year-old Stanley Roberts, evacuated to Southport with Bootle Secondary School for Boys, the radio was an important point of contact with his host family:

> The boy evacuated with me didn't stay long, so I was left on my own for the next seven or eight months. It was lonely, particularly the long, dark winter evenings. The highlight of my week was Tuesday evening when the man of the house, a quiet but kind man, would switch his wireless on and listen to Tommy Handley in the ITMA (It's That Man Again) programme – he would roar with laughter, and I would join in.

Rob Wilton, born in Everton, was also a popular entertainer with his catchphrase, 'The day war broke out', which was remembered long after people had forgotten the rest of the routine – 'My wife said to me "You've got to stop it" Stop what? "The war!" she said.' Rob's character joined the Home Guard in an attempt to comply with his wife's instructions.

Arthur Askey was also from Liverpool and had his radio programme with Richard Murdoch. *Band Wagon* was a pioneering programme, as it was the first radio comedy to put its performers into situations, rather than 'stand-up' routines. Arthur Askey had his own catchphrases, including 'Hello, playmates!' which was sure to appeal to children as well as to war-weary adults. As well as his popular radio appearances, Arthur also appeared in many films; during the war most of these films showed his characters getting the better of the Nazis. Films like *Back Room Boy* (1942) in which Arthur, on a lonely lighthouse off the coast of Scotland, outwits a gang of Nazi agents and *King Arthur Was A Gentleman* (1942) in which Arthur plays a soldier who finds an old sword, which he believes to be Excalibur, the sword of King Arthur. These films, and others like them, could easily be watched by whole families together, just as Elva Barooah remembers.

Younger children, or those whose family rarely visited the cinema, did not have visual images of war to frighten them. Junior cinema shows on Saturdays would not show adult newsreels. Very few people had television until the 1950s, as Evelyn Davies says:

> Of course, there was no television to see pictures of war or worrying scenes for us to have nightmares about. There was only wireless and the joy of listening to 'Children's Hour'. It was two old pennies to go to the pictures on a Saturday afternoon and our pocket money would stretch to that and maybe a comic or exercise book. Our expectations were not too high.

Shirley Landrum remembers that even when a child saw a newsreel, they tended not to be worrying:

> The only pictures I saw were when, not often, I went to the picture house called the Mayfair. There we saw Cowboy and Indian films, but before that there was always a news film. This showed us pictures of things happening in the war – these were always chosen to show how great England was. This helped everyone to put up with the shortages of everything without complaining much. We walked home in the dark, often our knees froze between socks and coat! We knew there was a price for everything. At home we had a wireless, it worked from a battery and a bottle of acid called an accumulator. One of my jobs on my Saturday shopping trip was to take the 'used' accumulator back to the shop, pay 6d and collect the recharged one. I knew it was dangerous and held it away from my body and dare not run in case the acid splashed me or my clothes. The wireless was important to my grown-ups; it gave important news. When they listened, we children dare not speak. Other times there were comic things on and we laughed.

Elva Barooah remembers Sundays as being different:

Sundays were excruciatingly boring as we were not allowed to play out. It wouldn't have been respectable – my mother wouldn't hang clothes out on a Sunday. That was as far as our religious life went – God wasn't mentioned – later, I went to Sunday School, as my friends were going. I wore my best coat and hat, handed down from my sister. That was just slightly less boring, but I didn't learn much about religion. On other days, we played hopscotch, ball games and skipping. I liked joining in but was really a reader! My father taught us chess and whist. My parents went to great trouble and expense to get us a china baby doll each. Their arms and legs moved. Neither of us liked them. They were too big to manage and they were always cold as ice. We adored cut-out dolls. Sometimes, they came in whole books – different figures with several tabbed outfits to put on – we could really play with those. We also had a small black doll, who was called Topsy, I'm afraid. We both loved her.

Topsy was a popular name for a black doll in the 1940s and 1950s, because it was the name of the little black girl in *Uncle Tom's Cabin* by Harriet Beecher Stowe, which most children had read.

Cut-out doll outfits or 'dress-dolls', as they were called, were provided with uniforms among the outfits with which to dress the cardboard dolls. Some books had titles like *We're All In It* or *Dolly Joins the Forces*. One title in this series of 'Up-to-date Story Books' was subtitled *Mummy Puts On Uniform*.

As the war progressed, toys, games, comics and books increasingly mirrored the events of the times. Comics like the *Dandy*, which appeared in 1937, and the *Beano*, in 1938, began to poke fun at the enemy with comic strips such as the *Dandy's* 'Addie and Hermie the Nasty Nazis' and the *Beano's* 'Musso the Wop (He's a Big-A-Da-Flop)', both the creations of Sam Fair. Desperate Dan, Pansy Potter, and Lord Snooty and his pals from Ash Can Alley frequently gave the enemy a trouncing. From September 1941 to July 1949, the *Dandy* and the *Beano* were published on alternate weeks because of paper rationing. These comics proved to be extremely valuable in brightening children's lives and they were psychologically worthwhile in turning a rather frightening enemy into a figure of fun. Nearly all wartime comics found their way into the salvage bins because their patriotic tone encouraged children to 'do their bit'. Today, this means that surviving wartime copies can be valuable in a different way.

The 'Biggles' series by Captain W.E. Johns included titles like *Biggles –Secret Agent* (1940), *Biggles Defies the Swastika* (1941) and *Spitfire Parade* (1941). *Worrals of the WAAF* (1941) and *Worrals on the War Path* (1943), also by Captain Johns, appeared, with a heroine who was the female counterpart of Biggles. Richmal Crompton's 'William' books included *Willam and the Evacuees* (1940) and *William Does His Bit* (1941).

But children did not spend all their playtime reading or listening to favourite radio programmes. Evelyn Davies remembers, when thinking of wartime pastimes, that 'just "playing out" with your friends came top of your list!'

Evacuation meant some relaxation from parental supervision and the opportunity for indulging in some harmless pranks. But Evelyn and her friend, Audrey Jump, found that being evacuated to Ormskirk, comparatively so near to home in Bootle, could be a mixed blessing:

Audrey's mother and mine would come on the train to visit us every so often. There was one day in particular that Audrey and I had decided to exchange clothes with each other, just for fun! She wore my gingham dress, which was way too short for her, and I wore – miles too long for me - her plaid skirt and blouse. The two of us were skipping along Derby Street, laughing at our daring for doing such a thing, when we were suddenly confronted with our mothers, walking towards us, on one of their visits. They were not amused, and told us to go back and change into our own clothes. Audrey's mother said we looked like refugees, and mine told us that our hair needed cutting!

Joan and Jim McMurtry remember happy summer days, 'We didn't go on holiday during the war, but had plenty of days out in local parks or across the river to New Brighton, Seaforth and West Kirby with a packed lunch of jam bread and homemade lemonade.' Pat Martin has similar memories. She was eight years old, with a ten-year-old brother, Alan, and they were living in Walton when the war began. At first, they stayed at home hoping that the war would soon be over, but:

> In December 1940, Liverpool was badly bombed, so Alan and I were evacuated to Eccleston to stay with friends of my grandparents. Every week Mum and Dad would visit us on a Sunday, and one week we begged to come home – just in time for the May Blitz.

Nevertheless, there was fun to be had. Pat remembers:

> We never had school trips, rarely holidays, but we enjoyed ourselves simply picnicking in the local park (Rice Lane Recreation Ground) with broken biscuits, jam butties and a bottle of water. Occasionally we went to the Pictures, which could be cut short by the wail of the sirens.

The local park also features in David Buckley's memories:

> In the war, we used to go to Sefton Park and there was a stage with lots of seats in front. It was closed in by railings about three feet high. I can't remember how much you paid to get in, but us kids used to stand around the fence outside and watch the show of different 'turns' – conjurors, dancers, singers – from there.

People were encouraged to take 'holidays at home' during the war years. It was, in any case, impossible to get access to most coastal areas and travel was discouraged. To make this idea more popular, local councils put on special events around the country. In the *Daily Post* of 17 June 1943, under the headline 'Holidays at Home' there were details of 'Next Week's Liverpool Parks programme'. This announced 'Open Air Shakespeare', with ticket prices of 2s and 1s, children up to age fourteen half price and continued:

> For the young folk, Wilding's Marionettes will be at Stanley Park from Tuesday onwards, with afternoon and evening shows. Concert parties continue twice daily in Sefton, Newsham and Walton Hall Parks, and there will be 'dancing on the green' at Sefton and Newsham Parks on Wednesday and Thursday evenings.
>
> Two local silver bands – Dingle and Kirkdale – give two performances each next Sunday in Sefton and Stanley Parks and on Saturday afternoon (June 26) there will be a Sports Gathering at Fincham Road, Dovecot, arranged by the Evening Institutes of the City.

At the end of the fortnight, on 6 July 1943, the *Daily Post* included this report in its column 'Day by Day in Liverpool':

> Open Air Shakespeare has been a decided success at Otterspool Park during the past fortnight. There were sixteen performances of 'Love's Labour's Lost' and the total of the attendances is estimated at about 15,000, an average of about a thousand for each performance. Over 7,500 paid for chairs.
>
> Last evening, the North-enders went to Walton Hall Park to see the first presentation of a play based on the legend of 'Robin Hood'. This is another feature of the Holidays-At-Home programme.

Some children did go away on holiday in organised groups during the war years. One of these was Austin Gahan, from Norris Green. His memories illustrate the contrast between war-torn Liverpool and the peacefulness of the countryside:

> We used to go camping to Ruthin sometimes. We were all in the Scouts. And the system was that every week we took tinned food to the Leader's house for our camping holiday. On the morning we went, we had to pack all the food into his furniture van. The tent was a large canvas sheet used by lorries, which was thrown over a pole between two trees. Going through the Mersey tunnel, we all had to keep quiet. When we arrived at the farm, the farmer's wife supplied us with bread and milk. When we pitched camp, it was lovely and peaceful. Mr Bernstein would take us on walks along the river into Ruthin. Our food was cooked on an open fire. What a wonderful holiday we had.

The Liverpool schools, particularly the grammar schools, organised extra-curricular activities. Frances Jennings, who went to Notre Dame in 1940, remembers those days with gratitude:

> During 1943, my interest in music and singing was helped at school, because we had an excellent music teacher who taught us to sing choral works, but to be in the choir, she tested each one of us and I was lucky to be chosen. My mother had a lovely tuneful singing voice and she sang many songs from her childhood in Ireland. She encouraged me to appreciate all kinds of music as a hobby. During this time, school concerts were held in the Philharmonic Hall in Liverpool which was not far from my school. These concerts were the idea of the famous conductor of music, Dr Malcolm Sargent, (who was later knighted) who sat at the grand piano and explained the music as it was played by the orchestra. It was my first introduction to 'Peter and the Wolf' and I was fortunate to attend many of these concerts afterwards. Being in the school choir gave me the opportunity to learn different music under the guidance of a good teacher and it became one of my hobbies, which I enjoyed and still enjoy to this day.

There were other community activities for children to enjoy or to take part in – amongst these were the Bootle May Processions. By the 1940s these were local recreational processions with displays and horse-drawn floats by local trades and firms. In most areas these were associated with Bank Holidays and in Bootle, one was held in May. Derek Finney was a page-boy in the Bootle May Procession of 1939.

This was an annual event, but after the 1940 event, it stopped for the duration of the war. When it recommenced in 1946, it was called the Bootle Carnival and had a Carnival Queen instead of a May Queen. However, in local parlance, it was referred to as 'the May Procession' until well into the 1950s.

Frances goes on to describe some of the out-of-school pleasures that were available in wartime, especially during the summer months:

> You could get a penny return on the tramcar, which took you to the terminus in Fazakerley, then walk to the bluebell woods and pick wild flowers. You could go to the Pier Head and if the ferry boats were sailing, you could go to New Brighton, stay on the ferry and return for twopence, as long as you were back for teatime. There was entertainment in all parks by Children's Dance Schools, who had the chance to show local talent. These were free for all people. The open-air swimming bath in Stanley Park opened in the summer; the boats on the lake came out, and, if you liked tennis, you could play on the courts (if the nets were still there). The boys could use the football pitch and Everton and Liverpool Football Clubs still played matches on Saturday afternoons. Street games were roller-skating, hopscotch, top and whip, skipping and ball games against the side walls of houses.

Bootle May Queen and Retinue 1939

Derek Finney, page-boy (right), in the Bootle May Queen's retinue, 1939. The other page-boy is Len Upton and the May Queen is Jean McKenzie.

Football matches had been resumed after their initial abandonment at the beginning of the war.

Other organised activities were also available. Shirley Landrum remembers a concert and the potential problem of costumes:

> For a while my sister, Glenda, and I went to tap dancing lessons on Saturday mornings. One day, Doreen, the big lady teacher with a lot of blonde hair, said there would be a concert. It was 'Alice in Wonderland' and most of us (untalented ones) would be playing cards. I grabbed Glenda towards the black cards side; I knew we had spare black-out material for our costumes, but there would be no chance of clothing coupons to get red. So we were black cards in the concert.

Back home from evacuation to Wales, Joan Tisdale, now a teenager, settled down to life with her widowed father:

> I was so happy to be back home. I settled down and joined the 'Girl's Cadets', which I enjoyed greatly. We learnt First Aid and we wore navy skirts, white blouses and a cute cap – it was called a 'Glengarry'. I was in the Guard-of-Honour at the Bluecoat Chambers in Church Street for the Duchess of Kent or Gloucester (I'm a bit unsure which it was), but we young girls were very proud, and we were given lemonade and biscuits, so we were well pleased!

Muriel Wrench, fifteen in 1942, began to have a busy social life in Prestatyn, where her family now lived. Her father travelled by train to Seaforth and back three times a week to manage the family business:

> A house was bought in Prestatyn. We had a garden. We lived on an unmade road. There were lots of families in the road whose fathers were in the regular Army, abroad with the Signals Regiment. Just over the sand-hills was a Holiday Camp, requisitioned by the Army and now filled with young recruits to the Pioneer Corps, much denigrated by the Signals! I was going to the Junior Red Cross First Aid classes. They were held at a soldier's Recuperation Hospital in Rhyl – fun but not likely to be much use. Bed-making with hospital corners. On Friday evenings I was also going to dances in the Camp – because it had been a holiday camp before the war, it had a ballroom – this was where I learnt to dance. I was lucky to have a mother who had worked as a dressmaker in Blackburn before her marriage and made our clothes. Dresses got altered and two fancy table-cloths became a blouse. Mum regularly went to the knitting group at the Camp. There were concerts given at the Camp, hilarious acts and sketches

and I also helped out at the local WVS canteen at times, but I didn't enjoy that. Because of the black-out, the kitchen was like a steam-room. Hair hung in strings. After leaving school, I went to a secretarial school in Rhyl. All girls and a longer lunch hour.

Muriel had not enjoyed school dinners, but found, after leaving school, that rationing still had its influence over what was available. 'The only disadvantage was the dinners – now to be paid for! We ended up going to every café we could find – from the British Restaurant where a shilling got you a very strange plate of food, and those butter beans still!'

The British Restaurants were run by the local authorities and some of them were very popular, with meals costing as little as 9d. Eating out was 'off ration', but at the introduction of rationing, people had been enraged at the spectacle of the rich eating well without coupons. From 1942, the government prevented any restaurant from charging more than 5s for a meal. The British Restaurant evolved from the London County Council's London Meals Service, which was a temporary way of feeding victims of the Blitz. In 1941, Tommy Trinder, a popular comic actor with great appeal across the social classes, was used in a short propaganda film, *Eating Out with Tommy Trinder*. This was intended to promote British Restaurants as completely classless, and communal eating as perfectly respectable. The idea of getting everyone together and people 'mucking in' was important to the government. In fact, the British Restaurants were patronised mainly by industrial and office workers, like secretarial student, Muriel Wrench.

Some of the remembered fun of wartime was impromptu, and the vicissitudes of wartime did sometimes bring about humorous incidents that have gone into family lore. Brenda Bryce remembers:

A landmine dropped outside 21, Peveril Street, in Walton, where we lived, and we had to leave the house while it was dealt with – so we went to Auntie Janey's house in Ladysmith Road, Fazakerley – but Mum already had a chicken in the oven, and rationing meant that this was a treat and not to be wasted, so Dad set off on his bike with the half-cooked chicken on the back of the bike, with we three (herself, her brother, Walter, and mother, Emma) following on the bus.

No doubt they were welcomed by Janey, her mother's sister, especially as they arrived with a half-cooked chicken. Brenda comments 'The smell was delicious!'

Bill Backshall, out looking for adventure during one air raid, had a lucky escape. One of the falling bombs in Lawler Street did not explode on impact, resulting in an incident, both dangerous and comic, long remembered by young Bill:

The unexploded bomb had buried itself under the front of a terrace house and out of sight. The residents were moved out and the area cordoned off with ropes, awaiting the brave bomb disposal squad to arrive, make it safe and dig the thing up. But they were very busy elsewhere. Came Saturday afternoon at three o'clock, when the local pub 'The Salt Box' ejected its merry customers. One of them was Mr McMahon, who had lost a leg in the First World War and would cheerfully tell everyone he'd been very lucky 'For it might have been my bloody head!', guaranteeing a good laugh. When, over-fortified with ale, he viewed the crater from the main road forty feet away, he ducked under the ropes and waving his crutches at it, shouted 'I'll dig the bloody thing out!' He staggered drunkenly towards it. Struggling down the roped-off hole he proceeded to throw out handfuls of soil, watched at a safe distance by a crowd of onlookers. Luckily he took the advice of the white-faced young policeman who cautiously approached him. Mr McMahon withdrew still waving his crutch at the deadly bomb and mouthing an old soldier's contempt!

Chapter Twelve

Victory and Peace at Last

Towards the end of the war, and particularly after D-Day – 6 June 1944 – school classes in Liverpool began to grow as the evacuees began to come home.

Barbara Yorke remembers her mother's involvement in the welfare of the returning evacuees:

> When my mother was widowed, she returned to nursing and, at first, for better pay, she went into private nursing, looking after a rich old lady, sharing the duties with a friend. The old lady died in 1940, so Mum went to what she had always wanted to do – work with children as a Health Visitor. Nearing the end of the war, Liverpool still had a lot of children evacuated and plans had to be put in place for their return. In some cases, families and children had kept in touch and so there should have been no problems. But, in other cases, the children had been away from their homes for a very long time with very little contact and they had grown up a lot and grown apart. Many came back to areas greatly altered and almost unrecognisable as home because of the bombing. Many could hardly remember their families. Some did not want to come home and some never did come home. Some foster families wanted to keep their evacuee and the child's parents, faced with a child who had become a stranger and did not want to come home, allowed this to happen.
>
> The Health Visitor was the first to talk to returning children. They had to inspect them and check for 'nits' and scabies and reintroduce them to their families. Fathers, in many cases, were still away in the forces, so the family was just Mum and, perhaps, Grandma. My Mum said that many of the children were very shy and she wondered how long it would be before they would settle down.

Peter McGuiness, ten years old when the war ended, remembers that:

> Classes at school were very large, between fifty and sixty pupils and, towards the end of the war, they increased as the evacuees returned. We were very envious of one boy who had been on a farm and operated a threshing machine. They spoke mainly with Welsh accents, but one or two spoke with Cumbrian or West Country accents. We mocked their accents but there was no individual hostility to them as cowards who had run away.

It seems that there was a national feeling of vague hostility expressed after the war towards those parents who had sent their children to North America or elsewhere in the Empire. The general attitude that it had been acceptable to send children to a place of safety but not to send them out of the country was probably reinforced by the Royal family's example. The Princesses Elizabeth and Margaret Rose, thirteen and nine years old when the war began, had, at first, remained at Balmoral after the end of the summer holiday in 1939, but later came to Windsor Castle, in order to be able to see their parents at weekends. They were there for most of the war years. When it was suggested to Queen Elizabeth that her daughters should be sent to Canada, she stated firmly 'They could not possibly leave without me. I would not go without the King. And the King will never leave.' The King and Queen were both known to have been practising shooting during the period when invasion seemed most threatening. Their example of steadfast and cheerful faithfulness to duty and quiet patriotism was a great morale booster.

Peter McGuiness recalls that the cinema was one place where children learned about the events of the war and realised that the end of hostilities was in sight. Even children whose parents did not discuss the war situation in their presence were likely to have gone to the Saturday matinee from time to time. Peter wrote:

> I was not a great cinema-goer… but I did go occasionally and it was from the newsreels that I learned about the war. At the Saturday matinee we always cheered wildly whenever our troops appeared. When the eighth army was advancing in North Africa and captured towns from the Germans, the first task was to pull down the German flag and replace it with the Union Flag. This always produced great cheering, especially when, in the process of change, the soldiers stood on the German flag.

Very few of the people who sent me their memories make any distinction between Germans and Nazis, as later generations have been encouraged to do. When they were growing up, there was no distinction.

Like the cinema, the radio and the newspapers were a source of information. For Eric Wells, twelve in 1944, who lived in Newborough Avenue, near Greenbank Park, D-Day was the beginning of victory:

> As the war progressed and the allies broke out of Normandy and started to advance into France, things became rather exciting. I recall lying on the floor at night listening to the 9 p.m. news to find out how the English, Americans and Canadians had advanced. I had a map of Northern Europe supplied by the 'Daily Mail' and small flags which could be cut out and the BBC pinpointed how far the war had progressed. When peace was declared, I think we were allowed home early from school. That evening there was a huge bonfire in Greenbank Park with hundreds of people about, and singing. That was VE day – 8 May 1945 – I was allowed up until nearly 12 p.m. A few months later, there was another bonfire in the park to celebrate VJ day on 15 August 1945.

David Rusling was born in 1939, and so his memories are mostly of the end of the war. He remembers the pleasure of experiencing some of the delights of peacetime that he had never known:

> My father had served in the RAF and finished up in Australia, so when he returned with many 'goodies' never seen before, including tinned fruit and, best of all, a toy cap gun. Around this time, I came across a strange item on display under a glass dome outside the old St John's Market. My grandmother told me it was called a 'Banana'. I attended three Victory parties, one in Romer Road, where my grandparents lived, one in Milverton Street, where I lived, and one at the Conservative Club in Durning Road. I did not start school until 1945 – I was told there was a shortage of teachers – but I do remember the day some men arrived at school and removed all the sticky tape from the windows and cleaned them. And then there was LIGHT!

In the later stages of the war, there were some relaxations to allow 'glimmer' street lighting, although not during a raid. But David's enjoyment of a lighter world was universally shared – there was great relief at the growing relaxation of the blackout restrictions towards the end of the war and, of course, utter delight when peace came and the blackout became a thing of the past.

After some time working at Owen Owen, Jean Campbell, who had once fallen from a tram during the blackout, changed her job, 'When VE came, I was Manageress of Martin's Cleaners in Wavertree Road. When peace was declared, along with my assistant, Lil, I shut up the shop and walked home.'

Joyce Jones, sixteen by 1943, was working in the Post Office Telephone Department in Old Hall Street. She remembers that:

> There was a change of scene on the dockside as the war drew to its close. We used to see the wounded soldiers arriving by ships at the docks, some on stretchers, crutches or in wheel-chairs. When the war was over, lots of men arrived back on the troop ships, often with bands playing to welcome them home!

Jim McMurtry, still only three years old in 1945, remembers the return of his uncles and his father from the war:

> At the end of the war, my Uncle Harry came back and said he and four mates had personally killed Hitler! And we believed him and told all our friends. And when Dad came back from the war, I ran to my Uncle George saying that a strange man was kissing Mum.

There were some unexpected and comical results of the ending of wartime conditions. Frederick Berwick, who lived in Kensington, points out:

> On the outbreak of war, the Government closed all the swimming baths to preserve power; consequently by the end of the war, those children aged around thirteen and under could not swim! When they re-opened, it was segregated swimming; everyone had to learn and because everyone was poor, no-one had swimming trunks, so they learned to swim naked. Eventually, everyone's Mum would make knitted ones (once wool was available) but you can imagine, they absorbed water and would reach your knees!

Patricia Blamire recalls the fate of her father's home-built air-raid shelter:

> After the war, my father had a brainwave. Why dismantle the shelter when it would be an ideal place to grow mushrooms? So trays were set out with mushroom spores and left in the dark. We waited and waited… nothing happened, so after a year, my father tipped the lot into the garden. The following year, we had a fine crop of mushrooms growing under our cabbages!

Elva Barooah, nine years old by the end of the war, who lived 'in a very respectable street', remembers that:

> At the end of the war the street next to us (which was considered a bit lower class than ours!) had a big children's street party. We didn't. Neither did the street on the other side of us (which was considered superior to ours!) I wasn't really disappointed… but my sister's friend, who was fifteen, was complaining we didn't put up any banners and have dancing in the street.

Frances Jennings remembers that:

Many street parties were organised and celebrations went on for many weeks, families were waiting for the troops to come home but it took a long time to happen. Some people had little to celebrate if relatives had been killed or injured. The fact that this awful war was over did not alter our lives very much; there were still many shortages… but life suddenly became more relaxed and the fear and horror of war was gone at last… as the years roll by, unpleasant things have a way of disappearing as the laughable and funny events take their place in our memory.

One soldier returned from war at just the right time; Sonia Part remembers, 'At the end of the war, we had parties in the street for both the VE and VJ celebrations. During one of the parties, one of our neighbour's sons came home from the fighting and what a welcome he got!'

Joyce Morley remarks:

Thankfully, the war ended in 1945… and the local neighbourhood congregated on a large field near to Childwall Abbey Church. People were so overwhelmed with joy that they stayed up all night keeping a huge bonfire going and dancing the night away to the strains of Bing Crosby and the Andrews Sisters, Glenn Miller and Harry James. Boogie Woogie was all the rage then. I don't remember much in the way of alcohol. I suppose there was a little but I was then fifteen and most of my age group did not drink.

Joan McMurtry says:

I have strong memories of VE day. There was, of course, a street party. Our upright piano was wheeled out into the street and the Vicar, a Mr Buckmaster, played popular songs, much to our astonishment! Roll out the Barrel; She'll be coming Round the Mountain and others! A good time was had by all with jellies and fairy cakes for the children, and games and races organised by the Mums and those Dads who were home. Our piano had beer marks on it ever after!

Pam Fawcett and her sister, Gill, have carefully preserved the certificate that the King sent to all schoolchildren at the end of the war. It is headed with the Royal Coat of Arms. Pam remembers:

The two photographs of the Victory Party were taken in Heliers Road, Liverpool 13. The two children together are my sister and I. We think our mother had to pay two shillings toward the cost of the party and we were given small ribbon badges to show we had 'paid up'. The other photograph shows all the children at the party from Heliers Road, Glen Road and Withnell Road, Liverpool, 13. It was a wonderful Day.

Brenda Bryce remembers the rejoicing through all the little streets off Breeze Hill, 'The VE and VJ parties went on for days – we kids had a total ball. Ate until we were sick and danced – danced – the streets were alive with music and dancing! However, nobody forgot what World War II cost some people.'

The wonderful spreads of food that allowed children who had been used to rationing to eat until they felt sick were the result of saving a little in advance, organisation and pooling resources by the women of the streets in which parties were organised. This planning went on for months before victory was declared and it was, in many ways, an act of faith. It was also an expression of the community spirit that had helped people to cope with the darkest days in wartime Liverpool.

Sisters Pamela Fawcett and Gillian Skinner, née Mylchreest, at the Victory Party, Heliers Road, Clubmoor.

All the children from Heliers Road, Glen Road and Withnell Road, Liverpool, 13, at the Victory Party.

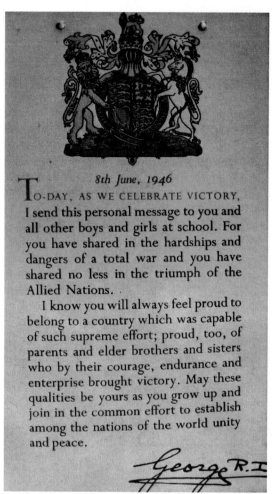

8th June, 1946

To-day, as we celebrate victory, I send this personal message to you and all other boys and girls at school. For you have shared in the hardships and dangers of a total war and you have shared no less in the triumph of the Allied Nations.

I know you will always feel proud to belong to a country which was capable of such supreme effort; proud, too, of parents and elder brothers and sisters who by their courage, endurance and enterprise brought victory. May these qualities be yours as you grow up and join in the common effort to establish among the nations of the world unity and peace.

George R.I

The message from King George VI to all the boys and girls at school in 1946.

Arthur Williams had returned from Colomendy in 1943, and he remembers that:

When VE day came, one of our neighbours put a piano on top of the air-raid shelter and everyone had a party with lots of singing and dancing. The same happened on VJ day. Although the war was on, everyone had felt safe; people left their front doors open… everyone felt they could trust one another because everyone pulled together.

Jim Williams agrees and shares his memory of the security of being part of a strong community; looking back, Jim remarks, 'We had a good feeling of togetherness. Everybody felt for their neighbour and that lasted for years. Sometimes I think I lost some of my childhood, but other times I think I gained as well.'

Liverpool's children look back on the war years with great courage and humour, celebrating what they learned through hardship, and recognising the closeness of family and community that were so important in those testing times. This is a generation of whom their city and their country can be justifiably proud!

Bibliography

Bradford, Victoria, *Joan Stables' Story* (Unpublished undergraduate dissertation for Edge Hill University)

Braithwaite, Brian, Walsh, Noelle & Davies, Glyn (1987) *The Home Front: the Best of Good Housekeeping 1939-1945* (Ebury Press, London)

Cheveley, Stephen (1940) *A Garden Goes to War* (John Miles Ltd, London)

Gardiner, Juliet (2005) *The Children's War* (Imperial War Museum, Portrait)

Keay, Mary (1990) *Memories of QM* (Published for charity)

Keane, Mary (1995) *Reminiscences of QM* (Published for charity)

Opie, Robert (1995) *The Wartime Scrapbook: From Blitz to Victory* (New Cavendish Books, London)

The Royal Horticultural Society (1943) *The Vegetable Garden Displayed* (RHS, London)

The Queen Mary High School Magazine, Jubilee Year, 1960

Other titles published by The History Press

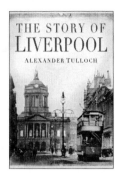

The Story of Liverpool
ALEXANDER TULLOCH

There is something special about Liverpool. From its beginnings it has always been associated with the ups and downs, the triumphs and tribulations of the rest of the country acting like a mirror to the events that have shaped the country we now think of as Great Britain. As one of the major ports in the land, Liverpool has witnessed the comings and goings of people from all corners of the world who, over the centuries, have constituted the melting pot of nations which has given rise to what we now think of as a typical scouser. Lively, readable and well-illustrated, this is a tremendous book for locals to enjoy.

978 0 7509 4508 0

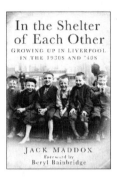

In the Shelter of Each Other – Growing up in Liverpool in the 1930s and '40s
JACK MADDOX

England is out of work. The mills are silent, and in the river, ships are rusting at anchor. The king is ageing and his successor remains unmarried. In Germany, Adolf Hitler has come to power. It is the wrong time and place to arrive in the world, but Jack appears all the same. A childhood spent in a bustling dockside pub in the roughest parts of the city and an early introduction to the school of hard knocks follows. Lawless, tribal and violent, but also exciting, humorous and generous; bonded by poverty, few had much, but nobody died alone.

978 0 7509 5102 9

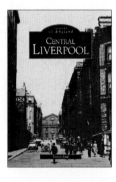

Central Liverpool
DAVID PAUL

This book of photographs not only depicts the cosmopolitan face of Liverpool but also the many changes that Liverpudlians have experienced over the last century. This isn't just a story based around grand buildings, it's about the ordinary people of the city as well. These people, with their indomitable spirit, have made Liverpool great and will make it great again. The photographs included in this selection dramatically illustrate the nature and character of changes in the city.

978 0 7509 0640 4

800 Years of Haunted Liverpool
JOHN REPPION

800 Years of Haunted Liverpool takes the reader on a tour through the streets, cemeteries, alehouses, attics and docks of Liverpool. Drawing on historical and contemporary sources and containing many tales which have never before been published, it unearths a chilling range of supernatural phenomena, from the Grey Lady of Speke Hall to the ghost of John Lennon airport. Copiously illustrated with photographs, maps and drawings, this book will delight anyone with an interest in the supernatural history of the area. *800 Years of Haunted Liverpool* is the first complete guide to the paranormal history of the region.

978 0 7524 4700 1

Visit our website and discover thousands of other History Press books.

www.thehistorypress.co.uk